NON-TOXIC ✳ ✳

✳ **NETWORKING:**

From Poisonous to Popular

more clients!

more customers!

more friends!

By: Jennifer Gniadecki

NON-TOXIC * * NETWORKING:

From Poisonous to Popular

more clients!

more customers!

more friends!

By: Jennifer Gniadecki

Dedicated to Randall

Thank you for supporting my dreams...even if you do complain an awful lot while you do. Oh, and for loving my sense of humor too.

ACKNOWLEDGMENTS

My favorite part of writing a book has been the people who have helped me. I have to admit, at first I thought writing a book was a one-woman job.

Was I wrong!

First, I'd like to thank Seth Godin. He said a couple of things to me that made me look away from the people I was examining to try and find what would make me happy, and look within myself for a truth that I knew and could share with others.

My editor Erika-Marie Geiss of Red Pencil Editing was beyond amazing. When I sent my book over, I remember saying to my husband, "I have no idea what editors do, and we may have just thrown our money away." When she returned the manuscript the changes were things I never would have thought of. It really improved the overall manuscript. I am amazed by Erika's work as well as her tenacity. She is an amazing woman.

Thank you to all of my business and personal contacts that love me and my quirky, professional personality. You have not only allowed me to be myself, you've enjoyed who I am. For opening up to me and showing me who you were beyond the facade and beyond business...I sincerely appreciate each and every one of you.

CONTENTS

PREFACE

I wrote *Non-toxic Networking: From Poisonous to Popular* because I keep watching people network badly. People are very, very ineffective at networking in most cases. I want to help each individual person but if I were to walk up to someone in a networking event and say, "Oh, hey, you really need my help with this!" That wouldn't make me any new friends and it certainly wouldn't open up a productive discussion.

Heck, it could get me smacked.

I don't want to offend people or make them feel inadequate. We are all wonderful and unique, but if I tell you what a beautiful, unique snowflake you are right after blasting your networking technique, you're not going to believe me. You might think I'm just saying you can be great to be polite.

After trying to help people one-on-one in a direct manner and having people think I was either insulting them or leaving the event with less self-esteem than they came in with, I decided that writing a book would be the most effective way to get the message out and help others make networking a more positive, meaningful experience. Not just meaningful for the networker, but more meaningful for the people that networker comes into contact with every day.

Not everything in the book will apply to every person, but I tried to include enough examples and enough different points of view to cover many, if not all, all of the personalities that will be out there networking.

With the popularity of the Internet, we see each other in person less and less. This creates two needs.

1. A real need to be able to communicate more effectively online, not only in the text we type, but in the words we speak. Each individual needs to find places where they naturally fit in, and then master the technology to speak to others online and work with an online conference room.

2. The need to not lose every social skill we ever had because we rarely interact with people physically. The more we are online, the less we are getting face-to-face time, and manners are getting left by the wayside.

If the only thing you do to improve your networking is mind your manners, you will have an edge over other networkers. If the most personal interaction you have with others is a drive-thru speaker at the local fast food restaurant, you need to get to a networking event as soon as possible. No matter what the state of the economy is, networking will always be the best way to get a job, a client, or a customer.

In times of a shaky economy, networking may be the only way you will find a job or client that pays enough to cover your bills – and it might be the only way to find customers and clients to keep your business afloat when people don't have as much disposable income.

I have made amazing friends while networking both online and offline. I am even the resident networking expert for an online forum of over 7,500 people. People at my local networking events don't know that, but it gives me credibility online. You can't assume your credibility will transfer online to offline or offline to online. Each space has different rules and different requirements to be considered an expert.

Your job as the networker is to find out what all the unspoken rules are of each group. Even if you're just out having a drink with your friends it is an opportunity for networking, just make sure your friends are okay with you being "on" for your business when you're supposed to be out for social purposes only. Some of your friends won't care, but some might, and you need to respect their opinion of networking as much as you might like to convince them that networking is the way, the truth, and the light.

I cannot emphasize enough that you always need to be networking. Even if you don't need anything, you need to always be meeting a few new people here and there for rest of your life. It can help in the most mundane ways...like finding a reputable plumber or a gardener or a dog trainer. But it can also help in dire circumstances. Where can I receive the most comprehensive cancer treatment? What children's hospital is the best? These are not questions you want to leave to chance and a phone book. You want to know from personal experience what people have been through and use that knowledge to save yourself valuable time and energy.

Your network is a valuable, special, living thing – with human beings at the other end of every phone call and every e-mail. Each one has a completely unique set of trials and tribulations they have gone through. While those experiences may help you in the future, those people may need your support in some way right now.

If you are being asked for a serious amount of help either emotionally or physically or financially, you need to be able to determine if they are just in a position where they need your help, or if they are the type of person that will take advantage of anyone with a kind heart and willingness to help. It's not a fun decision to make, and since I know that personally, I try to err on the side of being supportive. This may land me in a long conversation with someone that doesn't care if I'm me, or if I'm anyone else, or if I was a cat. But if that means

I never blow off someone that really needed my help, it is a worthwhile sacrifice.

There is great responsibility in effective networking. People will feel connected to you, care about you, and want to know more about you. Don't be shy, but don't share everything. Find a balance so you can further the relationships with people you would like to be friends with, and find a way to make and enforce healthy boundaries with people you don't want to be quite that close to.

Whatever you do, don't start sharing traumatic stories or deep, dark secrets willy-nilly with everyone you meet in an attempt to bond more quickly. You'll just be digging a hole that no amount of networking can get you out of. Use discretion, and if you need to talk about your serious or life-changing personal issues, seek professional help, not an ear to bend at a networking event. I hope that you find *Non-toxic Networking* useful and are able to take the information contained herein to evaluate and improve your networking skills in a positive way.

When you've done that you will find your networking is ultimately non-toxic to you, your business and your networking colleagues – and will result in more success for your business as well as your personal life.

INTRODUCTION
No really, don't skip this part!

Who is Non-toxic Networking for?

Non-Toxic Networking is for you. I know, that sounds cheesy but I promise it's the absolute truth. Success, both business and personal, can be skyrocketed using networking in an effective, focused way. So it doesn't really matter if you're looking for a client or for a date ▫ the tips in *Non-Toxic Networking* will get you where you want to be a lot faster than whatever you're doing now that may not be working so well.

> Networking will bring you more friends, more connections, and more opportunities. If that's not success...
>
> ... I don't know what is!

Even if you consider yourself a "seasoned networker," *Non-Toxic Networking* is for you. The way networking used to work doesn't work anymore. There has been a paradigm shift, and it is no longer about who talks the fastest or has the best elevator speech. What people want is more akin to the old general store – where they walk in and know who you are, ask about the kids, have a few moments of connecting before getting down to business. *Non-toxic Networking* shows you how to determine what you have to give and how to give it to others while retaining your dignity.

Who Non-toxic Networking Will Benefit

Non-Toxic Networking will benefit:

- Business owners
- Not for profits
- Independent Contractors
- Freelancers
- Mothers & Fathers
- Job seekers
- Anyone else that needs to make personal or business connections

I'm a business owner. As such, you'll that *Non-Toxic Networking* is written is from the perspective of a business owner. That does not mean it won't help you if you are not a business owner. Even if you aren't technically the owner of a business, your life is your business, and the pieces of your life (your career, your hobbies) are part of that and need to be given attention. When you give them the attention and care a business owner does to a business, other parts of your life will improve as well. No matter what your career path or business status, learning why networking works will have a positive impact on your life. Networking will bring you more friends, more connections, and more opportunities – if that's not success, I don't know what is!

What You'll Find in this Book

- The importance of appearance.
- How to be popular (no kidding!)
- Intention and how it affects networking.
- Branding (what it is and why you need it.)
- Different types of networking including online networking.
- Dealing with pushy people.
- Networking tools and resources.

So, if you see "your business" or "your brand" and wonder if those terms apply to you – they do. Just replace them in your head with "your job" or whatever applies to you so that the lessons make sense.

> We do a little self-analysis...
> ...but no one is psychoanalyzing you.

What Kind of Book is This?

Non-Toxic Networking is part self-help, part business information and no fluff. I'm not a big fan of the self-help book genre, and I did not intentionally write the book to have any kind of self-help element. It happened because the undeniable truth is if you don't have yourself straight emotionally you are not going to make solid emotional connections with others at an event. You'll share too much. Or someone will cross your boundaries and you won't know how to react. However it ends, it will end badly. So we do a little self-analysis – but only insofar as it will help you succeed out there.

I spent a lot of time in the business section of my local bookstore when I was thinking about writing Non-toxic Networking. There are so many books out there about business and improving your business. They all had one thing in common – they're filled with theory. They have these tidbits of wisdom and they explain some great overview of some great thing that some great business owner did this one time that made him a huge success. Unfortunately, they don't tell you how to apply that theory to your life, so if you can't make the leap from something that happened in the 1900s and make it relevant to your life and your business today...you're out of luck.

So many books on networking and business refer back to these early twentieth-century business leaders and talks about how they "figured it out" and how true success lies in retracing those steps they took.

What a bunch of hooey!

Sure, following someone else's path to success can yield great results, but what brings true success is finding a path that works for you. Just because Napoleon Hill and Henry Ford figured something out doesn't mean they figured out the only way – or even the best way. They were the pioneers of the Industrial Age...well guess what? We're not in the Industrial Age anymore. We're in the age where service and intellectual property are the tools of the trade and what worked for the Robber Barons and Captains of Industry a half century ago will not work for the modern day business owner or job seeker.

So why would you listen to someone that sold cars to tell you how to make your service-based business successful? Why would you listen to a Robber Baron to get tips on landing your next job? It just doesn't make sense, now does it?

What you need is a new way to succeed, a new way to make connections, and a new way of thinking. A new way that brings you more in *all* aspects of your life.

SECTION ONE
NETWORKING 101

"You have to care about other people

on a basic level

for anything in this book to work."

CHAPTER 1
Defining Networking

A Definition of Networking :

Dictionary.com defines networking as "A supportive system of sharing information and services among individuals and groups having a common interest."

It's no accident they don't specify business. Networking is any group of people with a common interest coming together and sharing information and services.

This means it is likely you are already networking and don't even realize it! If you are part of a book club, knitting circle, fantasy football league, or a group of dog enthusiasts you have a network.

Networking is, in its simplest form, having people you can call on. Did you make a new friend recently? They are part of your personal network. Did you meet someone that might know a great place where you can get a new job? They are part of your professional network.

If you need help determining who your professional network is versus your personal network, think about the people who know the most about your personal life. The people in your personal network are the ones that know the details of your love life. The people in your professional network know the details about the last big client you got.

If you only see someone at networking events, they are probably part of your professional network. If you're having a bad day or just feel sad or lousy, you should be calling someone from your personal network. When you want to do a post-mortem of your actions and the actions of others at the last networking event you attended, you should call someone from your professional network.

If you haven't transitioned someone from your professional network to your personal network already, don't use a horrible day or a tragedy to transition someone. It might backfire, and you'll find the person you're talking to feels put upon or uncomfortable being transitioned over to your personal network in this manner.

You can invite someone from either network out for a martini, as long as you know them well enough and it won't be construed as a date. You can also ask someone from either network to your next birthday party, as long as it's not being held at a strip club or that dive bar you happen to be fond of. Make sure you are putting your best foot forward when you're involving your professional network. You don't have to go all out, but make sure if you're inviting professionals to your birthday party, you're not planning on making a fool of yourself. The bottom line is people do business with people they like.

If you're not taking the time to get to know people and make connections with them, how will they know if they like you? Once someone knows who you are, they can pair you up with available business opportunities, parties, dates, or other people they think you will get along with. Once you start seeing this happen, it might feel like magic, but really you're just experiencing the power of being a person that takes the time to get to know others.

> Networking is any group of people with a common interest coming together and sharing information and services.

Some people are nervous about going to networking events because they feel that everyone is there trying to get something from them or is going to try to sell them something. Of course they are, you want something too, don't you? Be understanding of others who network as well as those who don't or don't realize they are networking. Even if people are pushy and rude about selling you something, try to be polite but firm, and always understanding. Not everyone has *Non-Toxic Networking*. Without it, they are not going to have the same techniques you will for being a hit. Everyone is at different levels when networking; and respecting those levels will only help you in the long run.

Sure we all want more clients, more customers, more money, more success, a better job – but to get those things you need to be a networking star. The way to become a networking star is to focus on *how* you network.

When you network properly and effectively you will be more memorable, you will be perceived as more giving, and that will make people want to give you more than they normally would.

Don't worry about everyone else's intentions. Worry about your own, because that is what will set you apart and make you an effective networker.

Why Network?

The number one reason to network is that you will not be successful unless you network □ period.

The best way to work your network is to keep a handy list of everyone you have met and what they do for a living. You can do this in various ways:

- Use an online web application.

- Put everyone into an Excel spreadsheet.

- You could enter everyone into an online or offline database program.

- If you don't have any of the above, you could even use a spiral bound notebook.

Make sure you put as much information as you have about the person into whatever system you use. Having this kind of list – either online or offline – will give you a referral network that can make you the "go to" person for others. Being the recognized person that can recommend businesses and service providers will make you the person people pick up the phone to call.

You want to be the go-to person so your name stays on the tips of tongues and in the front of people's minds. This is how you can become your industry's expert referred by others. They know you have been there for them and they want to do the same for you. By helping others solve business related problems you will be referred for your own services as well as for your contact list.

Why Networking Works

People love to talk. They especially love to talk about things they know well or have a passion for. Knowing what people want to talk about will set you apart from other networkers.

> The way to become a networking star is to focus on how you network.

Asking the questions that let people show you how much they know, how amazing they are, or what they are passionate about will make you the belle (or beau) of the networking ball. Everyone will want to talk to you, because they know you really want to listen.

On The Numbers Game

If you have all the right words and techniques in the world from every networking book out there, but are just looking to go through as many people as possible in order to score clients based on the law of numbers, you are going to come off as sleazy.

A quick and dirty definition of the numbers game: If you try and push your service on 100 people and one says yes, that means you need to talk to 1,000 people in order to get ten clients. You figure out how many clients you want, multiply by 100, and get out there and start forcing yourself on people at every event you can get to.

This does not work anymore. You can't just pretend you're listening in order to force a sales pitch on someone. Here is an example from someone in my network of how this can backfire horribly.

Julie was at a networking event talking to Beth and Daisy. Daisy had a habit of saying "doggone!" every now and then to emphasize a point. Julie wasn't really paying attention and one of the times Daisy said "doggone!" Julie popped her head up from her cell phone and said, "I got my dog groomed recently too, it was a nightmare!" It was obvious to both Beth and Daisy that Julie was not listening to the conversation, but was pretending to, by trying to catch one word and build her part of the conversation off of that word. Needless to say they then laughed about the story together and on the phone later to a few people each...who then told the story to their friends and as an icebreaker story to their professional network.

One conversation with someone pretending to listen, and now at least 20 people (probably a lot more than that) know that Julie doesn't listen. Julie is a real estate agent – would you want to work with a real estate agent who you've just been told doesn't listen? I know I wouldn't. That is potential business down the drain because Julie couldn't be bothered to listen to the conversation she chose to be part of.

You need to stop thinking in terms of pitching your product or service to the largest number of people possible. You cannot keep thinking that having a pitch and the "Lather, Rinse, Repeat" philosophy will eventually bring you great success.

Then again, if you're in my industry, I'm perfectly happy for you to keep doing what you're doing, because I'll just get the clients that you burn bridges with when they're still prospects. If you are plowing through people and pitching your business and trying to hard sell people without regard to the relationship, you are going to piss off every person you come into contact with.

Just because someone is shy and cannot tell you "No" - it doesn't mean to keep pushing until they give you a definite yes or no answer. Just because someone is polite, it does not mean they are interested in your product. Shy people, kind people and nice people - will all tell their friends you are awful behind your back if you act poorly. It is not an issue of being catty or rude. It is human nature. You're pushy. People don't like you, but they're too polite to tell you to your face, so they tell the people they trust so they don't have the same experience with you.

I've met women who are so pushy and oblivious and unable to listen to subtle hints and polite suggestions even I cannot bring myself to tell them how awful other people think they are.

If I told them, they would either flat out deny it or want me to help them fix it. I can't fix something that can only be fixed from within. I cannot give someone the desire to truly listen to another person. I can help with tactics and practical application, but that soul searching stuff is all on you.

> When you network effectively, you'll never wish you'd just stayed home.

Going beyond numbers and games

The flip side of this is that if you do take the time to listen and remember what others have said to you (best accomplished by making notes on that person's business card) and bring it up at another event as a follow up, you'll be surprised at how happy you can make someone when they see you cared enough to remember something important about them.

If you go into an event and show you really have a desire to learn about the other people at the event by showing a genuine interest in what other people have to offer...you'll be amazed at the results. When you talk to them about what you do, and are passionate about it, they will feel you are the expert about what you do and they *will* refer people to you.

You will also refer them to others for what they are good at. This is the give and take of networking. It's the balance of people sharing with one another so that everyone gets ahead and has access to resources within the network.

There is always someone worth talking to at any event, and you can always learn something new. When you are networking effectively, you'll never find yourself wishing you'd just stayed home.

The Importance of Intention

When I was a child, anytime I did something boneheaded I would try to explain it by telling my great-grandmother, "But Gram, I meant well." Her response was always the same, "The road to Hell is paved with good intentions."

The origin of that quote comes from St. Bernard in 1150, which is probably why we've all heard it at one time or another. In my opinion, it is this quote that has made us all what we are today...action based "do-do-do" type people. Intention is getting lost in the shuffle because the ultimate outcome of being solely action-based is that "the end justifies the means." This is not the way you need to be thinking if you're planning on making solid emotional connections with others.

Now everyone focuses heavily on actions and techniques and scripts and no one ever talks about the underlying intentions of networking (or sales, or marketing, or almost anything else.) This mindset creates a high-pressure, high-focus situation, and concentrates solely on what you do and the results you get. It turns networking into the dreaded Numbers Game where you're doing the math and cold calling and pressuring people into signing up or buying.

I am here to tell you there is a better, easier, non-toxic way.

You don't want to be the person people shy away from. You don't want people to see you and walk the other way or cringe and look uncomfortable when they think about meeting with you.

Understanding a little about how people think and feel, as well as having positive intentions behind your desire to make a connection will keep you from turning into a networking pariah.

Stop pushing people toward a sale with the hard sell. Go to networking events with the intention of making friends and sharing information. You will have much better results when you are well aware of your intentions.

You need to have positive, caring intentions when you use the techniques in Non-toxic Networking, or you will come off as cheesy and sleazy...and no one wants that. You have to care about other people on a basic level for anything in this book to work.

If you go into any networking event just to sell like a madman (or madwoman), and don't really want to get to know anyone, it will show. If you're all about you, it will shine through like a light in the dark, and you'll be left wondering why Non-toxic Networking works so well for other people and not for you.

Sometimes explaining or observing human nature and how people react to situations sounds a little sleazy. It sounds like manipulation. But if you are honestly out to help others, and you do it properly by getting to know who they are and what they do, that is exactly what people will see.

Knowing the outcome of your networking interaction before it happens makes you a wise and astute networker, not a sleazebag.

CHAPTER 2
Finding People to Network With

In Search of...

I talk about networking a lot. One of the most common questions is "Where do I find people to network with?" I understand the feeling, because at first everything seems so exclusive, and no one wants to become a paying member of an organization without first knowing a little more about how it works.

Basically what people are really asking is not "where do I find people" but "where are the people I want to know better?"

First, let me tell you something – you do not have to be a member of the Chamber of Commerce to attend some of their events. I have a friend who has been going to different Chamber meetings for the last couple years and she has yet to join. You can't attend special "member events" and you can't vote on officers...but so what? When you're first starting out you don't want that kind of responsibility!

As for other networking events, go to Google (or any other search engine) and pop in "networking events in (your town)" and see what comes up. You can search with the quotation marks or without you'll get many more responses without the quotation marks...that can be a good thing. If you live in a rural area, first search on your town then search on any larger towns within a half hour of where you live. Expand the search slowly until you find a few groups you might want to visit.

The key is to get to one, and talk to people and ask them what good events are in the area. Word of mouth is a fantastic (and probably the best) way to find networking events. Ask people you really get along with what and where their favorite events are and write it down.

When you're asking for these recommendations you can keep in mind that people hang around with people similar to themselves. I wouldn't use this to completely rule out a networking event, I'd just keep it in mind if it was recommended by someone you didn't get along with. You'll kind of have an inkling of what you're in for based on who told you about the event.

But don't assume that everyone at that event will be like that person who gave the event referral. Just don't be surprised if they are. Act appropriate and polite no matter how much of a bust you feel the group or event has been.

Everyone is a potential referral source and should be treated with the respect you'd accord to someone giving you business. That doesn't mean you have to talk to that person for four hours, make sure to get around the room to see if you can find someone you can make a real connection with, without blowing off or being rude to anyone. Keep it on an even keel and do your best to use every networking situation to build your business or career.

> Everyone is a potential referral source and should be treated with the respect you'd accord to someone giving you business...
>
> ...do your best to use every networking situation to build your business or career.

Who Are You Networking With?

There are some questions you can ask at any networking event. I've broken down some example questions into specific categories. They can be mixed and matched based on your personal comfort level with the questions. The goal of this section is to give you real things to say in real situations so you aren't reading a bunch of theory without actually being given anything to practice.

Eventually you will discover your favorite questions to ask, and which ones get the best response based on your networking needs. You can even make up your own questions. This is just a primer.

Here are a few general questions that work almost anywhere:

- **Can you recommend a good _____?** Show that you take referrals as well as ask for them. Only ask if you really are looking for something because the person will follow up and let the recommended person know to expect to hear from you. If you never call you look like a jerk.

- **What is your favorite thing about this group?** People love to give their opinion. Give them a chance to talk about the group you share by asking! You'll learn a few things about the group you may not have known before, giving you a feel for the people in the group.

Business Owners

Asking any specific company information can be seen as you trying to mine information or be a copycat, so make sure that when you use the following questions you do so in an open, friendly manner. Don't just ask and not share anything about your business – the reason these questions are so powerful is that you have to share what you're doing in your business or you will be perceived as sneaky. So share away, about how great your business is, what you do, what your plans are for the New Year, next year, the next five years...just make sure to do it cautiously and wait for them to share back before moving on. You don't want to get caught giving away the farm and not have anything to show for it in return!

- **How long have you been in business?** Only ask this question if the person seems friendly. You don't want to use this as an opener and have the person think you're asking to imply they seem new or unprofessional. But if you can use this question it is great because it can segue into....

- **Any new plans for this year (next year, the New Year, the holiday)?** Be prepared to share back if they answer. Don't give away your company's trade secrets, but have something prepared. You can be vague and still sound like you're sharing a lot. For example, "We're planning to market more on the Internet this year, how do you feel about that? I'm nervous."

> As with all of our tips, don't use these questions to pump people for information.

You are building a relationship; and the reason you're making sure that you are not giving too much away is because you need to have more of a relationship in order to determine if you can trust that business owner with more information about your company.

- **What made you decide to start your own business?** Sharing war stories is an awesome way to bond with a fellow business owner. It also allows you to see if your company is coming from the same general place as another business owner is. The war story that every business owner has is the moment they decided to stop working for someone else and start a business. That is because, for most people, starting a business is not something that has been done by everyone in the family. It is usually a very emotional decision, and is generally the business owner's favorite story to tell!

- **What would you say your biggest success has been this year (last year)?** People love to tell stories that put them in a good light. Plus, listen closely and you may learn something you can use in your own business.

How to Deal with the Modest/Shy Business Owner

You are networking, working the room, having fun, and you ask a business owner about their biggest success or why they started a business. You'll know you have encountered the modest/shy business owner when the response is, "I don't know" and they begin to immediately look around nervously.

If this happens to you reply with, "That's okay, I'm not trying to put any pressure on you." Smile so they know you're serious.

Follow up by talking about something that has nothing to do with business. The food, atmosphere, décor, whatever you can see or think of that isn't directly about business.

When you give the modest/shy business owner a chance to recover, but stay with them while they do, you will be rewarded by them thinking you are pretty darn nifty for not just blowing them off when they flubbed the conversation.

All of the modest/shy business owners I know have amazing contacts. Don't assume just because someone doesn't talk and isn't at ease that it means that they don't have amazing connections. Every business owner should be looked at for inclusion into your network on a case-by-case basis. Not based on overall assumptions about stereotypical information.

Women-only Events

Groups like the Professional Women's Network (PWN) and the e-Women Network are mostly (if not all) female. This means if you're a man, you can't flirt your way into business card heaven with these groups and others like them. (Not that I'm accusing everyman of doing that, I'm just saying most people have now and then.) On the bright side, women are easier to network with than men. Yep, I just totally said it. I'm being sexist, but just for a moment. Hear me out.

When you're at a networking event geared for women only, everyone feels a little safer. I'm not exactly sure why this is, but women at these events may seem cliquish but they're generally really open to meeting new people. They just tend to have the "game face" on that looks very "don't talk to me" – ignore it.

The compliment works wonders at the all women events because you can usually get a few women to chime in to give you backup on your compliment.

Like with any other networking group, when you're getting to know someone you need to find the sweet spot – the subject they really want to talk about. Once you've found that subject you'll be golden, and you can use portions of the story to tie into things that your business does.

Here are a few examples:

- **Family:** Be careful with this one. It can blow up faster than a '72 Pinto. You can make a vague statement like, "Any fun plans for the summer/winter/fall/spring?" Let them fill in family members at will. Do not assume they have husbands, kids, cats or dogs. These can all be emotional triggers.

- **Do you find all women networking groups have helped you in your business more than co-ed groups?** A straightforward question with not a whole lot of potential emotional baggage. Plus you can learn more about how women business owners network and if it is different than how the men you know network.

- **Do you know everyone here? There are a lot of women in this group. It must be very good.** You can act a little overwhelmed, because you probably are. We all get overwhelmed, even if we've been networking for years. Just be open about being nervous and perhaps you'll find a mother hen networker that will take you under her wing and introduce you to some other people. Be kind, be awesome, and try to remember as many of them as possible and get business cards where possible.

If you go to one of these events and you are one of those "all my friends are guys" women...it's time to suck it up and get over it. The things you hated about women in high school are just not as much of an issue anymore. Women are valuable members of society and formidable businesswomen. Being anti-woman is just passé. So yeah...stop that.

Executive Networking

There are some networking groups seriously difficult to get into. Only C-Level executives (CEO, CFO, and COO for example) and serious business owners have a chance to get in, and even they have to know someone.

You need to be on your game if you're at one of these.

- **Decide in advance what you want these people to know about you.** You don't know how much time you're going to get so make sure you have a concise point you want to make. If you offer 20 services, tell them about three.

- **Do your research.** Ask the person who has invited you to this chi-chi networking event about the people who will be there. Have her name names and companies. Then you do your research prepare a modified elevator speech that targets one of the people you've researched. Tell that person during your elevator speech what your company could do for them specifically. Conclude your brief talk with an open-ended statement of how you customize your services for every company and you'd be happy to speak to anyone after the meeting.

- **Be prepared to be flexible.** You need to know your stuff at an executive networking event. Know what makes you different, what you sell, how you benefit you customers, and be prepared to give examples.

- **You want to stand out.** Be friendly and remember that these people all get stuffy noses and stub their toes now and again. Treating executives and board members with humanity and kindness can get you far □ very, very far.

Group Networking

Almost all networking is, of course, in a group format. This section is more for very large groups of over 50. It can get difficult to keep track of everyone when there are that many people.

Remembering who people are can be a magic trick at this level of networking.

- **Have a pen handy.** The minute you get someone's business card write something on it about how you can help them, what they could recommend, or what they look like. (Be careful: Don't describe how they look in any potentially offensive way in case you drop it or anything happens that brings the card into a stranger's hands.)

- **Have a plan for who you want to meet.** You're there to meet people, so this is a great time to maybe go in with a cheesy yet effective line like, "You look familiar, I'm Jen...do you know if we know each other?" Even if they give you a scowl and say they don't think so...then just smile and say, "Then it's very nice to meet you, what do you do?" You can crack the veneer.

- **What's the group for?** If you are at a large group event everyone has something in common ▢ the group. Ask how long people have been members. The goal is to find the people you want to know in as little time as possible, while making people smile when you talk to them and not feel like you were playing the Numbers Game when you spoke to them.

Everyone is uncomfortable, not just you.

Lead Groups

Some people say these aren't technically networking groups because people come, exchange leads, and leave. But I like to err on the side of inclusiveness so I'm adding some tips. I could have used some when I started out!

- **Get there early.** Networking at a leads group tends to happen before the elevator speeches, not after the end of the meeting. Even if there is no networking beforehand, at the very least, you can score yourself a good seat if you get there early.

- **Don't get the buffet.** You're there to network, sure you can get a little something, but a buffet where you get up and down can be distracting. Also, you want to get something very easy to eat because you never know when you'll be called on to answer a question from a prospect. Don't order anything messy or that takes a long time to chew. Do not speak with your mouth full, and make absolutely sure you're chewing with your mouth closed.

- **Engage the group.** These people are used to hearing elevator speech after elevator speech. Mix it up and get people involved. Start with a question. "How many people here have a Web site?" if you're a designer. "How many people here have been confused in the last week?" for a life coach. You can use the answers to gauge interest and direct your elevator speech.

- **Use someone else in the group.** After the question is answered remember what someone that came before you in the speeches said they did. Now use your interest gauge and what one person does at the table to craft a mini-elevator-proposal just for that person. Everyone will see that you can think on your feet and that you can customize for individual people.

- **Relax, and don't be pushy.** Just try and enjoy yourself, the fast pace might energize you or it may make you nervous. Just try to make it through, get your message across, and don't push your message on anyone. It's not worth it. If people want to work with you, they will request more information from you.

- **Make sure you know how things work.** Someone invited you to the group, so ask them what the format is. (In other words, do your research.) Even if you've been to a group before, ask again. Just in case there are nuances for that particular group you've never experienced before.

> You want to look comfortable not like this is the first networking event you've ever been to...if you can help it. If you flub, so what, things happen. It's not the end of the world.

Grand Openings

Grand openings are wonderful networking events. The owners may have gotten a loan and have set money aside for just the kind of help your company provides. If you're looking for a job they just hired a bunch of new staff...you know someone isn't going to work out and will quit or be fired.

In both of these situations, the people you want to talk to are the owners of the establishment having the grand opening. They are going to need help in the future and you want to make an impression so you are the "go to" person when they decide it is time to get that help!

While you're waiting for your "in" moment with the owners, check out the workers and see what they do and who they know. You may know the other guests from around town already, but if not, ask them how they heard about the event or tell them it's great to see business owners supporting one another.

Just opening conversations can be great, because usually the people at grand openings are there for one of two reasons, the free food, or the networking. If you start talking to them...you'll soon find out which group they're in and can proceed accordingly.

Business After-hours

The Chamber of Commerce generally sponsors business after-hours events. The "business after-hours" gives people a quick opportunity to network as well as learn more about a local business.

The after-hours business provides drinks and snacks and people show up, partake of drinks and snacks, listen to a little presentation about the business, and network.

Don't go all nuts on the beverages and the snacks. Remember you are there for a purpose. Again, the goal here is to meet the owner of the company. They are there just to present the business to fellow Chamber members and visitors, and if you call them during normal business hours you would never get the same reception as you will during an after-hours event.

So take the opportunity and use the opportunity and bond with the business owners. Let them know what you do and who you do it for and how wonderful the snacks and beverages and the presentation was. If you can ask a follow up question from the presentation so much the better. You want to be genuinely engaged in the business and the owners so they will return the favor and will be interested in you and your business as well.

Chamber of Commerce Meetings

Even if you're not a member, you can still attend Chamber of Commerce networking meetings. You don't even have to go to the one in your town. You can pick a more affluent town, or just a different town. You don't have to go to just one Chamber either; you can pick your top five towns or cities and go to their Chamber meetings. This will allow you to get your name out there in multiple towns and not just in your home base. The more places that people know you without overlap, the better.

Just because you don't wear the uniform doesn't mean you aren't a great business owner.

Some things to consider about attending Chamber of Commerce meetings:

- **If you don't want to meet bankers, don't.** Chamber meetings are well known for having a couple tables of bankers. They all hang together, because they have a lot in common. If you want to meet them, go ahead, but if you don't want to meet bankers or financial advisors you will have to find a way to get out of conversations quickly and gracefully or you can get trapped for the duration of the meeting. One way of doing this is to say, excuse me for a moment I see someone I need to give a message to...and walk away.

- **Don't get intimidated by the suits.** Many people that attend chamber meetings wear suits every day. That's the business uniform. If you wear a suit too, great, but if you don't...don't let that intimidate you. If you are a suit-wearing business owner, don't judge people because they aren't wearing suits.

- **We can all learn from each other** and going into a Chamber meeting with an open mind can yield amazing results.

Formal Events

Going to a fundraiser? Going to a formal luncheon? Attending an annual award dinner? You need to be on your best behavior. This is not the time for lowbrow jokes because you think it will break the tension in the room.

The formal event is a chance for you to show that you can be taken out in public without peeing on the carpet like a puppy. This is a great chance to prove your company can hang in the big league. No matter how uncomfortable you are, you need to act like you belong there.

You can do this in a few different ways.

- **Having a plan in advance is crucial.** How will you deal with dinner? Where will you put your napkin? You don't have to plan every moment, but have the big questions answered *before* you set foot inside the event. Have your manners on point; read a book on manners or protocol if you need to. Find out in advance how many courses the meal has, and then make sure you know what fork to use and when. People notice little things like this, and you want to make sure that a lack of etiquette is not losing you potential customers.

- **Have a CD of music in your car** (or whatever else you need) that will put you in the mood to act like the prince or princess, king or queen that you are. Keep it together, and you will make a fantastic impression.

- **Don't be a snob.** You can still be friendly while acting like you belong at a formal event. You can still make people laugh and have a good time; just keep it appropriate for the event.

Online Networking Groups

There are many ways to network online. From LinkedIn to Biznik to the Business and Learning Expo and many others there are many ways to communicate with others in an online environment.

Each online environment has different rules and different ways of communicating. When you join a forum or a live, on-line text- or voice-enabled event, make sure to read previous posts or listen to what is currently going on to make sure you understand the tone of the group or forum before posting or the tone and subject matter of the conversation before speaking.

You don't want to accidentally offend anyone, and you don't want to ask a question that has already been asked a hundred times and get attacked for it.

Each group online has different people, and as such, a different voice. You need to know what the unspoken rules are as well as the tone of the group before you share your opinion or tell people how amazing you are.

Even the most knowledgeable expert offline comes online to a new venue as a new element. It is your responsibility as the new person to get to know people and make that bond with one or two others before you start telling people about your expert status.

- Squidoowww.squidoo.com

- LinkedInwww.linkedin.com

- Business and Learning
www.businessandlearning.com

- Facebookwww.facebook.com

- MySpacewww.myspace.com

- Biznikwww.biznik.com

(See the resources section for others.)

No one bonds with a braggart, and this is especially true on-line. Be gentle, be kind, be polite, and people will want to know more about you.

If you are part of an on-line expo or live vocal/text networking event, let other people talk and get a feel for the room before diving in. While each person in the cyber-room is still an individual, people who have been online for a while are more wary of strangers than people in networking groups where you meet in person.

That's because you can't see the person online and cannot make those initial judgments that people make based on how you look, how you smile, and if you seem safe and friendly. Often, all you are is text, and making sure you communicate effectively via text is important. Even if you can talk in the room and you have a microphone that works in the room, you need to make sure that you don't dominate the conversation. Give everyone a chance and make sure you are interacting with everyone as much as you can. Be friendly, listen to advice, and don't go overboard on trying to be an expert right out of the gate.

Figure out who the people running the forum, site, or group are and get to know them a little. Google them and see where else they are online. See if they are the kind of people you would like to get to know.

Meetup.com is a site that mixes both on-line and offline networking. You can get to know people with similar interests and meet in a public place and get to know one another better. From work-at-home moms to karaoke aficionados, there is a group for almost anything. There are a lot of business owner meetups as well. It will be your job to sift through and see if you think you can make better contacts with fellow business owners or if you should find a group that is part of your target market that is meeting up.

Be careful!

If you go to an event of your target market, when you introduce yourself don't give a big sales pitch or you will not be invited back. Instead, tell them you are there because you genuinely want to learn more about your target market, and that you're not trying to make sales from the group. In this way you are there for knowledge and the group might like having you there as someone that really wants to listen to their needs.

If being there and sharing and listening you make sales from the group, so much the better. But you have to be subtle about it, an "in your face" sales approach will only get you booted out of the group.

The Internet is fantastic and allows you to sell to people all over the country and the world. Used properly it can sell for you even when you're sleeping, and residual income is the goal of almost everyone I know.

Be good to your fellow Internet networkers, and they will be good to you.

Vendor Fairs and Trade Shows

Do you sell a product? Are you going to a trade show to sell from a booth or are you going there to meet others you can bond with and get tips and tricks from? Are you attending a home party of someone that has purchased from you before?

Some vendor fairs are more "crafty" than others. Some are high end jewelry. Some hover in between crafty and high end. Know what your product is and where it belongs.

If you are trying to talk to a business owner at a vendor fair or trade show, a surefire way to get the conversation started is by buying something from them. It doesn't have to be a big-ticket item, but you need to pony up and purchase something. This shows that you respect the time of the booth owner. While the purchase is being made, introduce yourself and tell them you've been looking forward to meeting them. Tell them how you heard about them and ask if they would have a few minutes to talk during a break, after the show, or during a slow period.

When you tell them who told you about them...make sure to add why they thought the booth owner would be a good resource for you. A little praise never hurt anyone.

If you are presenting at a vendor fair or trade show, take a minute during a slow period to talk to the other business owners at the show. Find out their experiences, how they're doing, and be friendly. You never know when a contact you make knows of great show down the road. They'll think of you because you spent some time getting to know them.

It is difficult to tell from price level who is someone to know. Just because someone has lower-ticket items they make and sell does not mean they don't have friends in high places. Don't judge based on a product's price point.

Random Daily Networking Opportunities

Don't overlook the opportunities that are in front of you every day. Just because the person in front of you at the grocery store is buying generic, it doesn't mean they don't own a thriving business.

> Remember, the worst thing that happens is you might accidentally make a friend instead of a business contact. Talking to other people and getting to know people in random situations can bring you more contacts both personal and business enriching your life in ways you never expected.

Just because the mom at the park is there in the middle of the day doesn't mean she doesn't know the person that you would love to get to know. She could have a business that allows her to take afternoons in the park. She could have a friend that is a CEO of a Fortune 500 company.

Other Random Networking Opportunities

- Starbucks (or Caribou, or your local coffee shop)
- The Hallmark store when you go to pick up a birthday card
- Community events in your neighborhood
- Park District programs and other kid's programs
- Reunions and other alumni events
- Commuter trains

You can leave your business card behind anywhere you go. (See the business card chapter for proper business card etiquette.)You never know who might pick it up, visit your website, and send you an e-mail requesting more information.

Make sure your friends and family know what you do and who you do it for. Prepare them for what to say if they run into someone that you could help. You can give them business cards to leave behind as well.

Even if you aren't a business owner, you should still consider having business cards and a Web site of www.yourname.com. Your site should have your résumé and any pertinent information you would want a potential employer to know about you.

Avoid putting your home address on the business cards or on the Web site. If you would like to receive mail somewhere, or think having an address on your Web site or business cards looks more professional, consider going to the UPS store and getting a mail box. When you get a box at the UPS store you don't get a P.O. Box number, you get an actual street address and if you have packages delivered, UPS will sign for them at your store location. Many shared office space or temporary office space companies also provide this service.

CHAPTER 3
Understanding Your Personal Brand

Cultivating Your Personal Brand

Large companies aren't the only ones with a brand, but they are a good place to begin when you are trying to figure out what *your* brand is. Every person should be cultivating a brand for themselves personally as well as for their business.

- **For a business** this helps people determine if they want to be your client or customer.
- **For an individual** it helps you come across in a way that will let people know if you are a good fit for this company or that company in your job search.

- Either way **it will help you**, as an individual, know what you are trying to communicate in every conversation you have while networking.

> Focus and clarity will help others remember who you are and what you do, and being remembered is the goal of networking.

Cultivating your personal brand helps keep you in the minds of others as an expert. This is also why your brand must be authentic to who you are as a person. If you have a brand that isn't true to you, it won't mesh with your personality and eventually you'll be telling stories or presenting yourself in a way that doesn't seem "right" to other people. They won't tell you it doesn't seem right, you just won't be getting any calls or emails.

- **If you are** a homebody, you cannot have a brand that is all about extreme sports. You'll end up in a conversation about extreme sports and say something like "but I'd rather spend the evening at home." No one is going to think of you as the extreme sports expert.

- **If you are** a work-at-home mom with absolutely no tangible or proven corporate experience as a mom, you cannot have a personal brand that pushes you as the expert for corporate moms.

There are different problems, and no one is going to see you as the expert for solving problems you haven't overcome them.

The technical definition of branding (from dictionary.com) is:

1. A trademark or distinctive name identifying a product or a manufacturer.
2. A product line so identified: a popular brand of soap.

These are a bit vague. A slightly more helpful definition is:

3. To impress firmly; fix ineradicably.

The purpose of your brand is to have you literally be seen as inseparable of what you do for a living. When you do this correctly, people never just think of you as, well, you anymore. Your identity expands in the minds of others.

You become:

- Jen the networking expert.
- Kathleen the boutique owner.
- Sarah the jewelry designer.
- Rooster the A/V producer.
- Sheila the bank teller.

This doesn't mean you're going to be completely pigeonholed into that one thing you're known for, if you decide to change careers or go from being an Internet marketing expert to an author, you can do that. The most important part of your branding is who you *are*, not what you do. The "what you do" part is secondary, but it is still important for referrals and business opportunities.

People that know who you are, but don't know what you do, cannot refer your services to other people. They will say "Oh, I might know someone that does that but I'm not sure." That will be that. You won't get the referral and that's probably the last time that person even tries to recommend you.

Don't let this happen. Know your personal brand. Here are a few questions that can help you determine your personal brand:

1. What are you selling? Is it your fantastic skill? Is it your creativity?
2. What problem does your product or service solve for the person that uses it? Does it give them more time? Does it make life easier? Is it pretty and fun?
3. What makes you different from others that provide what you provide? Why are you better? If you think you have no competition you are wrong and need to do more research, what other solutions are being offered to solve the

same problem. Just because someone does something different doesn't mean they are not your competition.

Armed with this knowledge about yourself and/or your company you can network more effectively. People need to know what you do, who you want to do it for, and what makes you special. When they know these things it makes it easy for them to make a recommendation for your company.

> It is your job to make it as easy as possible for other people to refer you.
>
> If it is difficult, people won't do it. It's just that simple.

SECTION TWO

DON'T BRING YOUR INNER CHILD TO AN ADULTS-ONLY NETWORKING EVENT

CHAPTER 4

The Popularity Postulate

On popularity

When you were young, popularity revolved around who you knew from childhood, what clothes you wore, what you watched on TV and talked about, and a bunch of other things that were controlled mostly by who your parents were and where you lived and some other random things you may have run across.

You're an adult now.

> Who you were when you were a kid or a teenager does not matter now....
>
> ...Take a step back from the person you used to be.

Not one bit. Sadly, though, your social standing as a child or teenager may be holding you back from networking effectively.

I find there are two major problems with popularity as it relates to networking:

1. You had a dismal life in high school. You didn't talk to many people and you were a nerd/geek/whatever and got teased and people said mean things to you. Basically things sucked when you were young and now you don't want to network because you're still carrying that monkey of uncoolness on your back.

2. You were cock of the walk in high school. It was the best time of your life. Everyone thought you were kick-ass and you thought so too! Now you're attending networking events and cannot figure out why people don't still think you're cool. You do all the right things, say all the right things, and people just roll their eyes and don't want anything to do with your company or aren't helping you find a new job.

Either way, you need to take a step back from the person you used to be. You've changed, whether you've noticed it or not. You need to reconcile the "old you" with the "new you" that has more life experience and more background and all kinds of other things that you couldn't have possibly had back in the day.

All the stuff you wish you knew then that you know now...that's the good stuff. That is the stuff you need to incorporate into your worldview for networking to really work for you. Those experiences and that knowledge are what make you special and unique and someone that other people want to know.

I'll let you in on a secret here, because I know you have to be curious about it. I have coached *just as many* people who used to be cool and can't figure out why people don't like them now as I have people who were made fun of and are still scared of how others will react to them.

The difference is the people who weren't cool in high school have this self-fulfilling prophecy occur where when people don't refer them they expect it, and the cycle continues. With the former popular kids, they are just genuinely shocked that no one wants to hang out and do business with them. Both paradigms are difficult to break out of because you're just so sure something should be true. When people are sure things are a certain way, it is difficult to break that belief.

So, let's focus on performing an honest evaluation of who you are *now*. Look at your strengths and weaknesses the way they will be seen by others as well as how you see them from a personal angle.

> There are some basic reasons that people don't
> succeed at networking.

The most obvious answers can be found by answering the following questions. Get yourself thinking about what you do when you talk to people you don't know.

Knowing the answers to the following questions will help you become more familiar with your strengths and weaknesses.

Here are a few questions to get you started:

- What is your biggest fear?
- If someone rejects you or doesn't like you, are they going to hit you? (no!)
- Are they going to make fun of you? (maybe – who cares?)
- Really, what do you have to lose?
- How do you ask for the sale?
- Are you cocky?
- Do you assume people want to know you and work with you?
- Do you talk a lot more than you listen?
- Do you even bother asking for the sale or trying to set a date for drinks or to connect again with a prospect?
- Are you telling your prospect how your product will benefit them, or are you telling personal anecdotes about yourself?

- Do you know what makes you different? Are you telling others?
- Do you assume someone will say no before you even talk to them?

Popularity as an adult may not look anything like you thought it would when you were in high school. That's because it's not high school. You do have to deal with a lot of people who haven't done any soul searching or used personal insight to grow since high school. But if you know who you are, you will be much better equipped to deal with those other personality types.

> ...if you're fat or thin, black or white, pretty or homely. Networking allows you to exist outside of that space.

Networking is a microcosm of society. The only difference is that when you're networking it doesn't matter if you're fat or thin, black or white, pretty or homely. Networking allows you to exist outside of that space. You can be in the networking space and be popular based on what you know, based on your business, your skills and what you have to offer. It allows you to make connections based on being human and vulnerable. No matter where you are coming from in your life, you can be a networking superstar.

CHAPTER 5

The Success of Personal Growth

Personal Growth

If you are one of the many, many people that still have the same hang-ups and issues that you did when you were in high school, you need to take a step back and address that. Even if you've crushed them down into a little pancake-like disc that lives in the back of your head in a box you never look in. They are affecting you, and you need to deal with those issues and get them behind you.

I know I said it in the last chapter, but seriously, it needs to be restated for emphasis. Some of you are thinking "Yeah, I know I need to do that, but...."

No buts!

You do not want your personal brand to end up being the neurotic person (or worse, the psycho). You won't get referrals and you won't get clients if you bitch about people having it so much better than you or if you say out loud that someone has more clients because they are prettier, skinnier, or have all their hair while you are rockin' a comb-over. By all means get rid of the comb-over if you have one, that's a sign of personal growth as well.

On Personal Appearance

While you do not have to be a model or a perfect ten to succeed at networking, it is imperative you take some time and pay some attention to your appearance.

When you wear a tie or shirt without stains, and you wear shoes that are polished, you are telling people you take care of yourself. Taking care of yourself for a networking event tells people you respect them enough to take a little extra time to look good for them. You don't have to get dressed up in a suit every time if that doesn't fit who you are or what you want to project, but if you wear jeans, make sure they aren't dirty and make sure they don't have holes in them. Keep yourself presentable.

You would not want to talk to someone who hadn't brushed their teeth or hair, don't expect others to forgive you for not putting any effort into getting ready.

Looking sloppy doesn't translate into being too cool. It translates into being sloppy.

Are You Being Bitter?

If you are standing in a group and you say out loud that you think someone else must be successful for ANY reason other than being a good business owner or being business savvy...you are going to find yourself on the outside looking in. You'll end up networking with other bitter people and you'll all wonder why you're not successful while blaming the success of others on something like looks or connections.

If you are blaming your lack of success in business on others you need to get your junk together and stop, because no one is to blame but you. If you are unpleasant, no one is going to refer you. If you are this person, use some common sense and change your tactics. Changing your tactics is the only way to avoid finding every door closing in your face one by one.

Afraid of People?

If it is a horrible, traumatic thing that happened when you were young (or even recently) that is holding you back – get therapy. If you're just still bitching about not being cool, get over it. How can you expect to run a business or focus on a real career when you can't even get your life together? You can't. You need to fix your insecurities and issues before you start networking.

It's a Small World

Unless you move, you don't get a bunch of chances to make a good first impression while networking. There are only so many chambers and groups. You get a few chances, and people understand that everyone makes mistakes now and then, but if you're consistently saying weird things or sharing too much too fast, you're going to find yourself very unsuccessful. That's because people like to know who you are and what you're about. If you're constantly sharing awful stories or complaining about others they think you're not good for referrals. You probably aren't, and being unprofessional shows the person you are networking with that you aren't even someone they want to know.

Most business owners hang out with other business owners that are like them. We all like to be around people who we have things in common with. If you are a loose cannon, if you are unconfident, your fellow business owners aren't going to want to be seen as those things and, as a result, are going to avoid you.

On Saying "No"

There are a lot of nice people in the world. That makes me very happy...usually. It only makes me unhappy when

I'm at a networking event and I watch a pushy person verbally bulldoze a nice person that can't seem to muster up the words "No, I'm not interested."

Many sales training programs teach that you need to keep asking until someone says "No," – "Um, I'm not sure" and "I don't know, I don't think so," or "Right now isn't a good time" don't count ▫they actually have to hear the word, "No."

Of course, this just happens, for most people, to be one of the hardest words to say.

I understand how you feel, you don't want to seem like a jerk, you don't want to be mean, you don't want to hurt someone else's feelings...blah blah blah...all those reasons and excuses for not saying that little word that will make all the high pressure sales stop.

Maybe you fear saying "no" is going to destroy any popularity you may have built up. Maybe I wasn't clear enough earlier when I said not to be abrupt. Maybe you just choke on the word. Whatever your reason for having the problem, you need to get over it. I know it's a rough thing to say, and that it's hard to do, but there are ways around it. For example, you can tell someone, "That product isn't right for me, but I'll make sure to refer you if I talk to someone that could use your product." The word no was never used and you promised them referrals...they may just say thank you and leave it at that.

But if they don't, it is your responsibility to say, "No." It's no one else's. To be able to network effectively and make solid connections, you'll need to know your own special way to keep the "pushers" at bay and not pestering you constantly.

Or you could even say, "I'm not comfortable talking about this anymore." Then walk away. You have to have enough self-esteem to know you do not deserve to have someone push you like that.

> If someone is pressuring you, and you cannot bring yourself to say no...just walk away.

On Being Pushy and Not Saying, "No."
A Horror Story

Lisa is a woman that my friend Dee met at a networking event. Lisa called Dee and said, "I really respect you for being really successful!" Dee said "Thank you." (What else was she going to say, right?) Lisa continued, "I'd like to come over next Wednesday morning, give you a makeover with my products so you can decide if you want to buy some. Once you buy some of the product, I'd like you to give me a list of all the salon, spa, and boutique owners you know so I can go and tell them you recommend they carry my product!" Dee said, "I have a 104 fever and that's not going to work for me." Lisa responds with, "I'll call you Tuesday night and see if you're feeling better." Dee says, "I don't think I will be, and I need to go lay down." Lisa closes the conversation with, "Talk to you Tuesday night."

Wow, right?

This is not uncommon. Especially with direct sales companies and network sales companies. I'm not saying you shouldn't be part of one of those organizations; your business is your business. I just know that some of the worst, most pushy sellers have come from being trained in these methods.

How could Lisa have been more effective? A few suggestions:

- Offer to bring over breakfast for Dee and a few salon owners and Lisa can give them free spa treatments.

- Offer Dee a free something, anything for the amazing leads Dee is providing for Lisa.

- Build the relationship before pushing a sale. Call and say "Hi, how are you doing?" now and then before calling and trying to force a sale and a list of referrals. Don't try and sell something every time you're on the phone.

There are many other ways she could have done better than she did in these circumstances. My friend is never going to give up that list to someone that offensive. Not in a million years. My friend cannot risk the relationships she has with the boutique, spa, and salon owners that give her business by putting someone so pushy in touch with them. When you refer someone that is annoying, pushy and rude, that reflects badly on you and your business. The pushy person will play up the friendship between the two of you and try to leverage that into a sale. The referral feels pressured, and may even worry you won't be friends with them if they don't buy from the pushy person. Now they feel that you, not just the pushy salesperson, have manipulated them.

You made your professional networking contact mad at you by making a bad referral.

The sad part is only my friend Dee and I know that. Lisa will never know about the pushiness and she will never realize that Dee isn't going to ever give up her contact list. This is because Dee just cannot bring herself to say, "No, I'm not interested in your product and won't be referring you."

So both Dee and Lisa are participating in less than ideal networking tactics, but you should always make sure you're not putting someone in a position where they feel that way about you or your product.

CHAPTER 6
The Problem with Shyness

I understand being shy. I'm an introvert that barely spoke a word until halfway through high school. Social situations make me dizzy with anxiety.

But you won't know it when you meet me.

Everyone thinks I'm this amazing "people person." They think I'm an extrovert. They think I was born with the gift of gab and humor and bonding with others. They think networking is very easy and natural for me. Remember what I said earlier about having overcome the problem you position yourself as an expert in solving?

I have learned not to let my shyness and anxiety get in the way of effective networking.

> Below every shy exterior are thoughts and feelings and opinions. No matter how shy or introverted the person, they still have something very valuable to give to the networking arena.

Being very honest about being an introvert, and having social anxiety issues, are part of my brand. People can't believe I still get a little nauseous on my way to a large event because I'm scared of encountering so many people! But I overcome it every time, and knowing that makes others feel better about being shy and introverted. That's why I do what I do. So we can all network more effectively – it's the only way for all of us to help each other become more successful in our careers and businesses.

If you insist on being shy at networking events...here is what you don't realize is happening.

A little scenario

The other business owners ask about your business (the polite ones that try to start a conversation) – you answer questions and then just get quiet waiting to see if they ask another question. Once the polite person runs out of questions to try to get you out of your shell they say, "Nice to meet you" and move on.

Why does this happen? You never asked them about what they do or who they are. You say it's because you're shy – but the other business owner just thinks you're rude. You know what? You *were* rude. By going to a networking event, you are making an unspoken promise to yourself and to the person holding the event that you will not stand there like a fool and do nothing but answer the most basic questions about yourself.

Sure you can just tell people you're shy, but come on. What do you do for a living? Are you a business owner? If you are, you have the personality and drive that are necessary to be able to put on your big-girl (or big-boy) pants and get over being shy. You can at least pretend not to be shy for the duration of an event.

Shy people that are incapable of dealing with other people become vets and deal with animals, they don't start a business. The same holds true if you are in any kind of service industry and are networking to get a new job. If you're in customer service, you can get over being shy. You don't answer the phone and say nothing, do you?

Really – if you couldn't do it you would have never picked up Non-toxic Networking. You know you have it in you. I have faith in you! You *can* do it!

On Not Being Very Shy
So you really are an extrovert, huh?

I hate to tell you this, but you are at a natural disadvantage when networking. I know I know I just went off on the shy people and now I'm coming after you. Well being an extremist isn't for networking events.

It's easier for a shy person to become a great networker than it is for a natural extrovert to become an effective networker. As a natural born extrovert, you have to learn to listen, to remember, and dial it down a few notches so you aren't completely overwhelming or scary to others. You've got to find a balance between you being high on all the energy of the room and finding the few people that are going to be real connections that can help you later.

Don't get caught up in trying to get the shy person out and talking. It's not worth it – they can only help themselves – find the people that are going to be of help to you and your business and find ways to help them get more business.

> This is how networking goes from being a meat market to being truly effective.

Shy or extroverted to the point of being obnoxious...either way you need to find a middle ground.

Other quirky personalities

Hi everyone else. So you're not shy and you're not hyper, huh? You should still take a few moments to reflect on how you interact with others at networking events. Are there things you could do to be more effective every time you meet someone new? Are there things you do now that aren't as effective as something else might be?

Sports teams always watch tapes of previous games to learn how they could improve the next time. Replaying a networking event in your head is a great way to go over what you did and where there is room for your improvement in non-toxic networking.

CHAPTER 7
Why are You Afraid to Connect?

Everyone has their own reasons and fears

The trials and experiences we've had through our lives have made us wary of making those connections with others until we've known them long enough to know we aren't going to get hurt. Or at least until we know the odds are low we'll get hurt.

> Being vulnerable is necessary for a quality relationship with another human being. All of us are afraid to get hurt, afraid to be rejected, not liked — all that stuff.

If you're going to be networking, you need to think of yourself as a professional gambler. But not the gambler that puts everything they own on some long-shot bet.

You want to be the gambler that uses logic and reason as well as calculating the odds to control how much you spend on each individual bet. (Do not confuse this with the Numbers Game.)You increase how much you bet over time based on the odds and the evidence you have at your disposal.

This way you can meet many people, but you're only investing a little in them at any given time. You don't meet someone and give them your life story in the first ten minutes. That won't work, and is too much of a gamble, and the odds aren't in your favor that person is ever going to want to talk to you again.

No matter what your quirks are, no matter what my quirks are, we are all afraid to connect to other people on some level. All of us are afraid to get hurt, afraid to be rejected, not liked — all that stuff.

Knowing why you are afraid can help you get over it and move on. It won't be fun to go back in your personal cache of ickyness, but it's the only way you'll ever be able to move on and not have the same hang-ups you used to have.

Sure you'll always be a little afraid, but it shouldn't be a deciding factor in networking or not. People are everywhere and eventually you're going to have to face the fact that you have to interact with them.

Unfortunately, now that you're reading this and you have actual solutions to how you can interact with other people better, you can't just throw up your hands and say, "I would, but I don't know how." You *do* know how, and it's up to you to take the first step to networking more effectively.

Also, be careful when you go to networking events of connecting with people who only have the same problems as you in common. Connecting on negative things could lead to you being really close friends with someone, but that friendship will be based only on negativity. You should always network with people who connect with you on positive levels, not just negative ones. Otherwise you and Negative Ned will go to events together and you'll be two people, petrified to connect, except to people with the same issues as you.

You'll end up being a gang....but not a fun gang like in *Sex in the City*. It will be more like a depressed, creepy gang that no one wants to hang with.

CHAPTER 8

The Stupidity Supposition

I cannot count the number of times people have said to me, "Networking makes me feel stupid." That feeling like your feet are too big, you don't know what to do with your hands, the whole nine yards of feeling like a big dork.

Guess what?

Everyone else feels that way too.

Everyone at some time or another has felt stupid while networking. You can pretty much bet on a couple of people at every networking event you go to are feeling like they'd rather be beaten up with big sticks than be there. You can usually see it on their faces, and it is sad because they probably go home and wonder why no one wanted to talk to them, thus reinforcing the stupid feeling.

The best way to get over feeling stupid is to be prepared. Yes, it's that simple. The anxiety comes from not knowing what is going to happen, the fear that no one is going to like you or want to talk to you. The only way to effectively get past feeling stupid is to get used to the feeling, which is the first step to getting over the feeling entirely.

It helps if you have your revised elevator speech handy so you know what to say when people ask what you do.

Have your compliments handy so you can begin conversations and be seen by others as friendly and outgoing.

If the networking event you are attending requires you to stand up in front of anyone and talk about what you do, remember what someone else said and engage that person. Point out how what you do matches with what they do and let the other members listening fill in the blanks for their own businesses. You can't connect with ten people at once (not right off the bat anyway) so why not focus on connecting with one person. It is not only more effective, but far less stressful for you.

If you have decided that you don't want to network in a setting where you have to stand up and talk to a group of people, that's okay. If standing up in front of a group makes you nervous and you suffer from that "I could never talk in front of a group" feeling, it is your responsibility to check in with the networking event organizer ahead of time to determine how they network. There are many kinds of networking groups and you don't have to attend ones that make you feel uncomfortable. If you don't feel good, it will come across to everyone that you're having a very negative experience. Until you feel ready to tackle that kind of event, skip it.

If you didn't check with the organizer and you find yourself in a situation where everyone stands up one by one and gives an elevator speech, you cannot say "pass" when it is your turn. Do your best, don't go on too long, and sit down. Trying not to give an elevator speech at all or avoid talking about your business is basically the equivalent of making a scene.

Don't do it. If you *must* "pass," there are three options you can try. First, make a quick exit ▫ either go to the bathroom or sneak out and claim illness later. Second (and the best option), is to suck it up and say two sentences about your business. The third and fun option works only if you're there with a friend or colleague. Try and convince them to talk about your business for you. Of course, you're going to have to talk about their business for them in return, because each person can only talk about one business ...but it's always easier to talk about someone else's business than your own...so give it a shot. Your friend talking about your business will make people listen, because you're doing something different from everyone else. You'll also find out if your friend knows what your business actually does. This will help you understand how other people hear it when you explain what your business does.

> Ultimately, if your bad feelings about networking are stronger than your need to be successful, get clients, get a better job...or give up now. It is better to make no impression than a negative one.

You're better off not networking at all if you are just going to go into the room looking like you have been forced to be there at gunpoint.

If you just need help getting through your negative feelings about networking, get to the bottom of what's making you feel bad. Ask yourself:

- Why do you feel stupid?
- What is the worst thing that can happen?
- If that "worst thing" happened, what would you do?
- Are you okay going through the rest of your life being afraid of connecting with other people?
- Can you visualize, fantasize, or daydream that you are the most popular person in the room—the person that *everyone* wants to network with?

The answers to these questions should help you get an understanding of what you fear and how you can get past it. Just because I know that every human being is capable of effective networking does not mean a darn thing if you believe even more strongly you are not capable of doing it.

SECTION THREE
MAKE THE MAGIC HAPPEN

CHAPTER 9

The Networking Buddy™

The Networking Buddy™

While you are still in the phase of being scared or uncomfortable, your first order of business is to find just one person you can go to events with so you are not all alone.

You can find this person at a networking event by asking what other groups they go to and asking if you can tag along next time. If you're scared of going to your very first event call up a friend and ask them to come with you. Either way you're going to feel more comfortable knowing you have someone going with you. You'll already know someone, and that means you have an excuse if you're talking to someone you don't want to be, or someone to talk to in between networking with other people, so you never find yourself standing against the wall feeling uncomfortable and looking like a deer in the headlights.

My preference would be to see you hook up with someone at a networking event and go with them to the next event. By "go with" I don't mean drive together. Meet them there. That way when you walk in you'll be looking around for someone you know, and that will ease your entrance transition. You have someone to meet and you look like you have a purpose when you walk in the front door.

The Networking Buddy™ is also fantastic because this is how you find networking groups you couldn't find on your own. Every person has their own set of groups and people they tend to hang out with. Introducing yourself into one of these groups is a way to go into new situations as someone who is already known. You never again have to walk in and wonder who you should talk to first. Start with your Networking Buddy™ and ask them who you should talk to next.

Then when you find that person you can start with, "Oh, so-and-so told me I should talk to you because you're amazing at _____" You have a reference name and a compliment. That is powerful stuff, and the person you've just walked up to is going to want to talk to you.

Remember, you're not the only one who likes to go into a networking event already knowing someone. Even the most seasoned networkers like to know they will know someone at the event before they go. It is human nature to not want to venture into a group alone. It makes everyone feel more comfortable more quickly, so don't worry about being a third-wheel, you are helping them as much as they are helping you.

Just make sure you don't attach yourself to your Networking Buddy™ like glue and never leave their side. They are a mental security blanket, not a physical one. They exist to make you feel better about being there. They do not exist to stand right next to you all night. You can also cross refer to your Networking Buddy™ by letting people know what they do while you're networking. "I came to the event with Yamisi; she is an amazing Virtual Assistant, have you had a chance to talk to her yet?"

Talk to your Networking Buddy™ before the event if possible to see if they want to cross-refer with you as well. The worst that can happen is they only want to promote their business. The best that can happen is they will think you are a genius for thinking of how to work the room twice as fast, and twice as effectively, because a referral is always more effective than an advertisement.

A note for the guys: If you can get a Networking Buddy™ that is a woman (who is *not* your significant other) that will go a long way. It will show to others in the group you can have professional relationships outside of your own gender. It isn't necessary, but every little bit helps, especially if you are trying to market toward women.

Having a woman cross-promote with you at an event will be taken much more easily than you talking to women who are wondering if you are hitting on them or trying to sell you something. If you think that is happening, a female Networking Buddy™ may be just what you need.

CHAPTER 10
Six Things

The Six Things

There are six main things you need to know before you network. This is in section three because it is the beginning of the planning section.

> You need to write these six things down...

You need to write these six things down and put them up on a corkboard in your office, or put the answers on post-it notes and put them on your monitor. Put them wherever you can in order to see them at least once a day. You need to be focused. The easiest way to focus is to keep your six things right in front of you.

1. What are you selling?

You need to know what you are selling. If you sell jewelry you are selling beauty. If you sell handbags you are selling style. If you have a Virtual Assistant business you are selling time.

What does your company sell?

2. What is your biggest fear?

Are you afraid people won't like your style? Are you afraid people aren't going to understand your work style? Are you afraid you won't be able to show your product to its best advantage?

Everyone says their biggest fear is not getting customers, but the fear of not selling comes from somewhere else. That reason (and understanding it) can help you tremendously in more than just the networking aspect of your business.

3. How have you asked for the sale in the past? How's that tactic working out for you?

Are you asking for the sale at all or do you just figure that the person will ask you to buy your product or sign your contract? Is that working? Whatever you do to close a deal, analyze how people react to it and make a determination. Does that work for your business, or should you be looking to revamp your closing?

4. What is your BIG goal?

If you network for the next twelve months, what is your big huge dream goal? Is your goal to make enough money or get enough clients to go on a cruise to the Caribbean? Is your goal to acquire enough new business to budget for a Virtual Assistant so you can do less of the administrative work and spend more time networking and selling? Is your big goal to grow your business enough to sell it and live the rest of your life on a small private island? Whatever your goal, know it. You need to know what you're doing all this work for!

5. How does your product or service benefit your customers?

Jewelry benefits a customer by making them feel more beautiful which in turn others will notice as the person wearing it actually looking more beautiful. Marketing Services benefit a customer by letting them worry about producing the best product possible because the marketing company is selling that product. The benefit is the freedom your product or service gives your customer. The benefit is how your product or service makes them feel. It is entirely emotional.

6. What makes you different from your competitors?

You need to be able to tell potential customers in a diplomatic way why your product is the best. Being the best means you know you are better than other products. It is a fine line between explaining how great you are and trash talking another company. You should avoid trash talking at all costs, because it doesn't make you look good. Focus on being "most" Are you the most value-based company? Are you the most fashionable? Are you the most eco-conscious? What is the key element to distinguish you from the competition? Highlight it.

CHAPTER 11

The Networking Plan

Networking Plan for the Business Owner

If you are a business owner, you probably have a business plan. You may even have a marketing plan. Hopefully these things are written or typed somewhere in a file. Perhaps you even read over them now and then and see if revisions or changes need to be made.

For the sake of your business, I really hope you look those documents over now and then.

But back to networking – I am the only person I've ever known that had a real live written down networking plan. Why is this? People have always been taught to network by showing up, making small talk, passing out business cards...and leaving.

If that was all I did I wouldn't need a plan either.

But you're not planning on networking like that, are you? I didn't think so. You've seen a better way□a way that leads to more referrals, more friends, and more fun.

So here is what we're going to do. We are going to put together a networking plan for you right here, right now.

First, you need to know what you're looking for:

- More colleagues?
- More referral partners?
- More friends?
- More clients?
- More opportunities?
- Better party invitations?
- More publicity?
- Joint venture opportunities?
- Business partnerships?

These are all things that networking can provide, but if you go in wanting everything without a plan or process, well, it is going to be a lot more difficult and take a lot longer. You may not even succeed, because you don't even know what success will look like unless you get some elusive everything from your networking efforts.

Knowing which of these you are aiming for will help you hit your target every time you attend a networking event. You can pick more than one, but saying "everything" is just too vague.

Now that you know what you want, you need to know how you are going to get it:

- Meet complimentary business owners that will be good referral partners based on the niche of your businesses.

- Meet people that want to start a new business but need someone with your skills and expertise to be able to succeed.

- Meet speakers and find out how they moved from consulting to being a professional speaker.

- Find one reporter or journalist or someone that works in print media in the room to make a connection for potential publicity.

These are all things that networking can provide, but if you go in wanting everything without a plan or process, well, it is going to be a lot more difficult and take a lot longer.

Then have a goal for each event so you know when you have succeeded:

- Schedule lunch with a reporter.
- Schedule coffee with a speaker.
- Schedule a phone call with a potential business partner.
- Make the acquaintance of a referral partner.

You can change your goal and tactics for each networking event or you can keep doing the same one until you feel you've become comfortable with the process of achieving your goal at a networking event.

Have prepared questions for the people on your goal sheet, so when you do meet them you have things to talk about other than just your big goal, because if you just talk and don't give them something to talk about so you can listen – it doesn't go as smoothly. So have questions for the speaker ready, like, "What experiences did the Chamber find valuable when they chose you as the speaker for this event?" You'll get information you find highly valuable, and at the same time the speaker gets to talk about their experience.

Everyone likes to talk about what makes them special, and asking why the entire Chamber felt that person was special is going to elicit a good response and an honest answer. That can benefit you as well as potentially make the Chamber speaker a Networking Buddy™.

Networking Plan for the Job Seeker

If you are looking for a job in a certain field, your networking plan can be to find people in that arena, and ask them about the experience and how they would recommend someone find a job like that. It doesn't have to be complicated; you're looking up to them as employed when you're looking to make a career move, so they will feel like they are mentoring you in a sense.

CHAPTER 12

The Entrance

Why It's Important

Now that you have your ducks in a row, and are rocking your networking plan, let's go over the importance of the entrance at a networking event. While the entrance isn't the most important part of an event in terms of networking power and how other people judge you, it is important. It can set the tone for the rest of the event and can make the difference between you feeling prepared and excited or nervous and horrible for the rest of the night.

> These are all things that networking can provide, but if you go in wanting everything without a plan or process, well, it is going to be a lot more difficult and take a lot longer.

In most cases it is best to go to a networking event with a buddy. It can be a Networking Buddy™, a friend, or anyone in your contact list that has a good personality. Don't invite the weird loud person just so you're not alone. Who you hang out with directly affects how others judge you.

If you're still new to networking and don't know anyone at the event, the tips in this section are even more important for you. It is imperative you put yourself into a good mood, and be in a good place mentally *before* you walk into a room full of strangers to convince them you are fabulous. First thing you need to remember – you <u>can</u> do this.

Everyone at the event is human, has cried, or has had a horrible day. You don't know by looking at someone if they've been mugged in the last week or were told by a spouse they want a divorce. Don't assume you are the only uncomfortable person in the room, and by all means don't assume you are the least successful.

Getting in the Mood

There are many ways to get yourself into a positive mindset on your way to a networking event.

The number one thing I make sure of when I'm going to a networking event is to have great music in the car. I made a few networking CDs that I always have in the car just waiting for me to pop them in. By the time I am at the event venue, I'm dancing in my car flipping my hair and I feel like a superstar!

Do you have songs you listen to that make you feel amazing? Put them on a CD to listen to on the way to a networking event. You'll feel great getting out of the car, feel great on your way in the parking lot walking toward the event, and it will stay with you all the way inside. People will see you are happy and smiling and they'll want to talk to you.

Sign in at the front door, smile and say hello to the volunteers if you have to sign in. Then walk through the door into the mix of things just knowing that everyone is going to be thrilled to talk to you!

> Put on your favorite lipstick, carry your favorite wallet, or wear your favorite shoes.

If music isn't your thing (hey, it happens!) there has to be something special you can do, or something amazing you can wear to make yourself feel fabulous. Do you have a special necklace? Do you have a pair of lucky undies or boxers? Wear them! Put on your favorite lipstick, carry your favorite wallet, or wear your favorite shoes.

Do whatever it takes to make you feel like a million bucks. If you do these things, it will shine off of you like a second skin and people will pick up on it. When you're in a good mood, you walk taller and with greater confidence. It's a physical manifestation of your internal feeling—so just get into the groove. Other attendees will want to know who you are and they will come and talk to you. If you go talk to them, they'll be much more receptive to finding out about you and what you do.

Judging on Appearance

Many popular articles say that you should picture your ideal client and then when you enter a networking situation, try and find that ideal client and talk to them as soon as possible.

I cannot think of worse advice.

First of all, I've noticed that just because you're dressed well or presenting an aura of success doesn't mean a darn thing. Usually someone talking about how successful they are isn't that successful at all. Bragging tends to be a sign of huge insecurity.

People know me most anywhere I show up, so I wear a nice shirt and nice jeans and comfy shoes that aren't sneakers. I do not fuss and fret over my networking wardrobe. I own my own business, and am known for my Internet expertise...why on earth would I wear a suit? There is no need, and that's not part of my brand.

Are you a knowledge worker? If you have information that people don't generally know, it helps to dress down a bit. You will be seen as more approachable and less intimidating. People would be freaked out if I showed up to a networking in a suit and started talking about how to integrate your branding and marketing efforts on the Internet and started talking with industry jargon and above people's heads...you get the point. I'd be seen as a know-it-all and unapproachable.

The key is to get your message across (no matter what you do) in a way that makes the person you're talking to feel interested. This means not looking scrubby and unkempt, but it also means that you need to dress so that your clothes match your message.

If you dress in something that makes you feel good you will make a better impression than wearing a suit and feeling uncomfortable. Of course, if a suit makes you feel like you're on top of the world – by all means, wear it! I'm not anti-suit, I'm just against wearing things because you think it is what you should be wearing. Wear it because it represents you. Be yourself.

Wallflower Syndrome

After picking out your favorite outfit, putting on your lucky undies, and listening to awesome car tunes...don't blow it by being a networking wallflower.

If you've networked before, you can look around and usually see one or two people standing completely still and looking around like they wish they could run out of the nearest exit.

Don't do this. Please. You need to enter, take a quick scan of the room and do one of two things:

1. Find a fellow straggler and say hello. They are as desperate to be part of a group as you are. Oblige them.

2. Find a group that has an incomplete circle and get in there. Not all groups are comprised of perfect circles and people will naturally include you if you fill the gap. Especially if you have the attitude that you belong. (You got that attitude with your car tunes and lucky undies, remember?)

3. SMILE. Not the fake "I work at Disney" smile. Think of something positive, happy, good and wonderful and have a real smile on your face when you approach people. They'll include you. Smile with your eyes. If you have to, go ahead and think of something really happy that's not the networking event. Use the memory of a pleasant, happy event in your life to conjure up a good, real smile.

Ok, that should get you from your house and into the event. Now you're in and you've walked up to someone. What do you do from there?

CHAPTER 13

Express Yourself

Communicating

Networking is all about communication. So now that you're inside of a networking event and you find yourself walking up to someone or a group of people...what do you do? You need an icebreaker and the perfect icebreaker is a compliment.

You need an icebreaker.

It is the "old faithful" icebreaker that you can use no matter what the situation.

The Compliment

The number one, never inappropriate, sure fire way to start a conversation in any networking event is the compliment.

In some cases, people have trouble giving compliments. They feel uncomfortable giving and receiving compliments. The whole thing just feels weird and wrong. If this is the case for you, you're going to need to practice giving compliments in non-networking situations to get comfortable...because if you're not using the compliment to begin a conversation you are giving away a lot of good leads and good conversations when you don't need to be.

Most people love getting a compliment. Even people who don't believe the compliment or slough it off or deny it or don't take it well. Have you ever had someone compliment you and you said "oh pshaw, this old thing?" and then the rest of the day you felt a little lighter – a little brighter – because someone noticed you and felt strongly enough about something you had to compliment you on it?

Practice

When you practice, you should start with the friendly compliment. This is just a random compliment you give to someone you know.

- Tell your mother you like her purse.
- Tell your dad you like his new shoes.
- Tell your sister you like her new haircut.
- You can practice complimenting anywhere!

In many cases the person you've complimented will blow it off or not take your compliment the same way they might if someone else complimented them. That's okay, you need to get used to it. Just remember, it does not mean they don't appreciate the compliment just because they don't thank you for it.

Once you've gotten used to complimenting the people you know, move on to strangers. This is a little harder, but if you've been practicing on loved ones, you'll be prepared. I've never had someone look at me funny for complimenting them. I've never had anyone think I was crazy or weird. People can sense your intent and if you are just giving a compliment for the sake of a compliment, the person you are complimenting will register that.

You can start in the line at the grocery store. Compliment the person in front of you. Find something you actually like, and say you think it's nice. You could say, "I love that scarf, where did you get it?" or "Your handbag is really chic." It just has to be something you'd really say out loud. If you use words like chic, go for it! If you don't, now isn't the time to start...it might sound funny. You're already trying new things by complimenting others, why add new words in the mix? Don't stress yourself.

Friendly Compliments and Networking Compliments
There isn't a big difference between the friendly compliment and the networking compliment, but there is a difference. You are using the networking compliment to say hello and begin a conversation.

It is designed to disarm the other person from thinking you are just another person selling something or trying to get a job. You aren't there to use them, and they shouldn't feel that way, and if you use the compliment you put them in a friendly mode instead of a defensive mode.

The biggest difference between the friendly compliment and the networking compliment is that when you compliment the person at the networking event you **never** ask where they got something.

Correct: "I love your handbag!"

Incorrect: "I love your handbag, where did you get that?"

When you ask where someone got something, the answer they give you will be the end of the conversation and you will feel awkward moving on from there. In time you may not feel awkward, and can use it. In time, and as you network more, you'll be able to turn that type of question into a networking opportunity and should use it, but for now, avoid it, unless you really want to know where they got the item you're complimenting them about. In most cases you want to let them thank you for the compliment and follow up with something like, "Oh, by the way, I'm Jen...nice to meet you!" and smile and laugh – they are now much more open to knowing more about you because you just made them feel good. Use that opportunity to let them know a -*little* bit more about you and end with a question about them, so they have time to talk about who they are and what they do.

After the compliment, focus on letting the other person talk to you more than you talk to them. Before you know it you're having a real, live conversation that started out with no hassle and no uncomfortable moment. You can't beat that!

Combining the Entrance with the Compliment

To be effective from the outset of a networking event, combine the entrance with the compliment. Pick an individual or group and walk up to them. Don't speed walk, that can be a bit scary, just walk up to them normally. When you walk up to a group, pick someone. The best way to pick who to compliment is go for the first person you see something really nice on that you would like to compliment.

Make sure you are about to make a compliment on something you genuinely like. Do not just pick something random. You have to be able to give a real compliment, not a fake compliment. If there is a gap in the circle, walk into that gap and compliment the person on your right or your left and that will solidify that you belong in that spot.

Don't just start complimenting everyone willy-nilly or they'll think you're lying. Even if you pick something real to compliment on each person, too many compliments will make you sound sleazy (or that you think it's a pick up bar not a networking event) so keep it simple.

One person, one compliment, one introduction.

Then listen to what everyone is talking about. Is it something you are interested in? Do you want to know the people in this group based on what is being talked about? If it isn't, say excuse me to the person you complimented and let them know you'll be back later and walk away.

Yes, you *can* just walk away. You may have picked a group that's a dud. You may not like what's being talked about. This is a networking event and it is okay to network. The only way you can do that is to experience different groups.

The bonus? Now you know someone. Who? The person you complimented and introduced yourself to. This person can be used as a wingman/wingwoman later if you need one. You now officially know someone at the event. If that person changes groups you can go to the new group they are in and say, "Hello again. We were both just over at 'X' group," and mesh right into the new group. If you do this, make sure to get their name this time if you didn't last time!

The Networking "Hello" and "Goodbye"

The compliment can be seen as your networking "Hello." It is something you say to each new person you meet. It needs to be different for each person, mix it up. You can even bring other people into the compliment to create a new group.

To create a group, you find someone, and then compliment them by saying, "Oh wow, I love your scarf." Then turn to the nearest person and say, "Excuse me, don't you think her scarf is lovely?" The other person will, of course, agree, and now you can begin talking to both of them. Violá! You've created your own group in a networking event. There is no reason to feel weird. Everyone at the event is trying to meet new people without looking weird.

Most everyone I meet loves meeting new people. Well, they don't like the actual "meeting" part, but after that initial awkwardness ends, they love knowing someone new. Knowing new people allows you to have people in your network that see the world in different ways than you and can show you a different perspective from what you're used to. You can actually become smarter by the virtue of knowing and talking to more people.

So you can see why getting over the creepy-weird feeling of breaking the ice is important for so many reasons. Make it easy for people to know you and you drastically increase the chances they will like you.

The big issue is not necessarily meeting people. It is that many people don't know they had an impact on your life, because you don't tell them. If you want to be a super-networker, you have to be able to say "thank you" to people you network with.

Even if you're already utilizing the compliment as an opener, even if you're meeting lots of people and they all enjoy your company, if you want to seal the deal and actually see networking connections become friends you still also have to say "Thank you."

The "Thank you" is just appreciation for some information or thing that the person you're talking to said or made you think about. They are spending time with you, and that's a gift they are giving to you. They deserve to be appreciated for it.

Some examples:

- "Thanks for letting me know, I'll think of you every time I hear that now!"
- "That story really touched me. Thank you."
- "Your honesty is really refreshing. Thank you.
- "Wow, I never would have known that if you hadn't told me, thanks!"

> The compliment is your hello,
> the thank you is your goodbye.

You should be finding a way to say thank you to every person you meet and have a conversation with. The compliment is your hello, the thank you is your goodbye.

Everything in the middle should be building toward your goal, and the goal of learning about the person you are talking to, but if you don't say your networking hello and goodbye you are not going to make the impact you desperately need to in order to get what you need from the networking experience.

It may feel a little weird at first expressing appreciation out loud for a bit of information or for telling a great story, but the rewards it can bring make up for feeling a little weird. You're doing something that most people just don't do. You will stand out, and in a positive way. That's why you're networking, right?

On the Friendship Identity Crisis

When you are networking effectively, you will make emotional connections more quickly than you are used to. You may notice people are calling you a friend that you barely know. People may start calling you just to chat when you've met them one time.

You need to be aware that many people are not used to having emotional connections with people that aren't already-established, long-time friends. So when they feel that feeling, they associate it with being friends with someone. If you made them feel connected to you, they now think you are friends.

Do *not* tell them they are not your friend. (Yes, I've heard people do this, and it is bad form!) That is going to create bitterness and resentment, because you will hurt the other person's feelings if you tell them that. What you can do is determine if you would like to be friends or stay acquaintances with the person and act accordingly. You don't have to tell them they are only an acquaintance, but you also don't have to return every phone call immediately. You can have emotional distance without ruining the bond. Just remember to be

polite, but keep your boundaries strong, or you are going to have too many friends and not enough business connections.

It is okay if people think you are so like them that you may as well be siblings that were separated at birth. You need to be comfortable not getting sucked in and keeping the level of friendship where you need it to be based on your networking goals.

Of course, it is entirely possible you are so similar you're like siblings separated at birth. If that's the case, BE friends. It is okay to make friends too...just don't make friends if it isn't what you want from the person.

Just don't let someone else dictate your life. Maintain whatever boundaries are comfortable for you for each situation.

CHAPTER 14

Boundaries

Boundary awareness

Being unaware of boundaries is another common mistake that networkers make. I'm not talking about inching your plate and utensils or personal space here, you have to be aware of how much you are sharing with another. Even if you feel comfortable, that's not the time to start talking about your atrocious childhood or your dog that got hit by a car when you were seven and destroyed your belief in God.

It is also not the place to brag. You have to strike a balance between being seen as a scary psycho and über stuck-up. There are appropriate circumstances to tell almost any story you have. It is your job as the networker to make sure you're not creeping out the person you are talking to or making them feel stupid because you are more knowledgeable than they are.

Even if the person you are talking to tells you a disturbing, traumatic story...do not respond in kind. You do not know who at the event is a gossip, and you don't want your dirty laundry aired for everyone to know about by the time you go to your next networking event. While some people are genuinely sharing, others use their own "trauma" as bait—so be careful.

Keep your trauma to yourself.

If you feel you may not be able to do this, call up a therapist and tell them. If your trauma doesn't directly relate to your business or to your brand, keep it under wraps. It's just not necessary and again, it might get around and you could have complete strangers knowing your personal drama.

No one wants everyone to know who they are because of something horrible that happened when they were 12.

There is a delicate balance of trust between networking acquaintances, especially if you get along really well and start talking about families and pets and hobbies. You have to remember why you are there and remember there are a lot of people in the world that don't have friends and really want them. Don't get sucked into a two-hour personal conversation at the networking event with someone that's telling you about their trauma.

> You need to make more contacts—that's your focus.

If you really want to let that person talk more about personal stuff, schedule a time to have lunch. Don't waste the networking event talking to someone you barely know and letting them tell you things you don't necessarily want to know.

I have had people tell me the most amazing things within an hour of knowing them. Once, a powerful downtown lawyer basically told me he was in love with my client's mother. How weird is that? I have no idea why he told me that, and it disturbed me to no end, but I just politely got off the phone and moved on with my day.

Boundaries – Yours, Theirs, Ours

When you are a good listener, people are going to tell you things. Many of them will be wonderful, engaging stories. But other times they are going to be sad things, depressing things, gossipy things. You have to know where your boundaries and comfort levels are for those kinds of stories. You need to know up-front what you can handle and what will freak you out. When people find listeners, sometimes they want you to just sit...and listen...for the rest of the event.

If this happens to you here are a few tips for getting out of it graciously:

- Get someone walking by to join the conversation. This is a great time to bring back that wingman/wingwoman you complimented at the beginning of the event. Or anyone else you've complimented during the evening.

- Tell the person that you would love to continue this conversation at a later date, and to give you a call when they have time and you can talk or schedule a time to have lunch together at a more private place than a networking event.

- Say, "Wow, I really respect your courage in that situation. Now I need to come up with a tenth of that courage and talk to someone that might be my next new client. I'd hate to miss this opportunity even though I'd rather hang out here with you."

As long as you make an effort to be tactful about the situation the person should let you go. If they are a nutcase and refuse to let you go, you just need to walk away.

I know, I know...you're a nice person; you don't want to just walk away from someone in pain. Look at it this way - they've probably told a hundred other people about this, you are not special. They are telling a traumatic story at a networking event, and you could be anyone. So let it be someone else.

To stay and listen and convince yourself you *had* to listen because no one else would is totally ego-based on your part. If it will make you feel better, after you break away keep tabs on the storyteller. They'll have someone else sucked into their web of trauma before you know it. You'll see that you really weren't that special to them.

It's okay that you weren't that special. You do not need that kind of drama in your networking!

Knowing Your Boundaries

Now that we've gone over people attacking you with their personal problems within what may seem like ten seconds of meeting you...we have to go over one other kind of networker that you will need to defend yourself from.

You walk into a group, compliment someone, start a conversation, and all of a sudden you're being overwhelmed with questions. Where did you grow up? Where did you go to school? Do you have brothers and sisters? You are probably initially pleased, thinking that this person's interest is genuine and they may become a client, or at the very least a great referral partner.

Then you realize that the questions are getting more and more personal and you've already answered so many it would seem rude not to keep answering. So you end up telling her some of your own traumatic experiences, some disappointments, the state of your business (for good or for bad) and where you hope to take your business in the next five years.

You realize this person practically has your business plan as well as enough blackmail material to last about a year. Then she abruptly stops talking to you and walks away.

Feeling violated and used, a little dazed from the experience, you look around to see that she's talking to a group of people and gesturing in your general direction. Not only did this person pump you for information, the information you just gave is being used to bolster that person's social standing within the group!

This is not a fun situation. I've heard from people this has happened to that it can bring a grown person to tears. It really is shameful someone would do this to you, but you don't need to worry about other people. You can save yourself from this situation by knowing in advance what your limits are. Most of us assume the best of people, but realize that not everyone has the best intentions.

That being said, knowing your boundaries *before* you go out networking is very important. Some things may not be a big deal to you – number of siblings, if you're married, if you have kids. But your business plan? Your five-year plan? Those are not anyone's business but yours.

> Most of us assume the best of people, but realize that not everyone has the best intentions. If you tell someone you aren't having the best year...you don't know who else is going to hear that.

As much as we would all love to trust everyone, you cannot tell people your business plans willy-nilly! You don't know who that person knows, or if they will literally steal your idea and do it within their business. Or if they have a friend that is a competitor and you don't even know it. Now they have your plan and the person can pass that information on to the competitor and they can either steal your idea or counteract it with a plan of their own.

Usually business espionage is not a big thing. It's the little things said over cocktails here and there. If you tell someone you aren't having the best year...you don't know who else is going to hear that.

You may have clients pull out for no reason and they won't tell you why. Only that "it's just not a good fit anymore." No one wants to sail on a sinking ship – even if your ship isn't sinking – they have information from a "reliable" source that you said you weren't doing well.

People twist things for any number of reasons. So it is your job to make sure the information you are giving out is innocuous. Set your limits in advance and you will know when it is time to answer a question with a smile and a simple, "That's a company secret." Even if the person pushes, once you've said you aren't going to answer once it will be even easier if they say, "Come on ... you can tell me!" to reply simply with, "I'd love to, but not even my husband/dog/kids know that about my company. I just have to keep it under wraps for now."

Even if that makes your questioner less than happy, you've been polite and they can't go back and say you were being a jerk about it. The worst outcome is they'll tell people what you said with a, "Who does she think she is?" To which everyone in her group will reply silently that you are someone they want to know.

Mystery is a beautiful thing, and having a little in your business is a great thing. Not how you run your business □ that should be no mystery. Even what you do, unless its classified, shouldn't be a secret. But your plans, your marketing, how you advertise, what your niche is – may all be things you don't want to share, and you don't have to.

Just remember, you're the only one looking out for your business and you need to treat your conversations that way. Keep your company in a good light, if it is doing badly right now focus on one or two positive things and just don't go down the path of negativity.

If someone starts a conversation with "Business has been so rough with this recession, hasn't it?" Just smile and say, "I'm sorry to hear you're not doing so well, I hope you can get that turned around." Do not even engage in a discussion of how well (or not) your business is doing.

In most cases the recession argument is just used as an excuse (recession or not!) to pump the other business owners for information. The person I knew that used this line was actually very successful; he just used it to find companies his could buy out.

> If you tell someone you aren't having the best year...you don't know who else is going to hear that. Do not even engage in a discussion of how well (or not) your business is doing.

I'm not saying you have to be worried and paranoid and not trust anyone. Quite the contrary, I believe you should trust everyone to an extent until they prove they do not deserve that trust. But don't give them everything you have the first time you meet them. Leave some for a second conversation, and if you bond as well as you hope, there will be time for that second conversation where you can tell a little more than you did the first time.

Make sure you are aware of the things that happen during a conversation that should be considered "Red Flags" – things that should make your brain take a moment and say, "Be on the lookout for trouble." Trouble may never come, but if you get used to the things people might say when they are being less than honest it can put you in a place where you don't find yourself saying something you regret the next morning.

The Boundaries of Others

> Now that you're aware of the problems that can arise from someone else being an oaf at a networking event, let's make sure you don't become the oaf.

People have pretty obvious signals to tell you when they feel uncomfortable in the conversation. The gaze of the person you are talking to might wander until you begin to wonder if there is a bird on the roof or something else taking the attention of the person you are talking to. They're looking everywhere but at you...you need to wrap up or ask them a direct question so they re-engage in the conversation.

The yawn is a painful but obvious signal the person you are talking to is done with the conversation. Even if they cover and apologize for yawning and say they are still totally interested, you need to move on. Even if they are interested, someone in that exhausted of a state is not going to remember what you told them. You don't have enough time to spend it on someone that isn't going to remember what you were talking about.

If all other signs point to interest and the yawn is a weird aberration, you can suggest you walk and talk simultaneously. Depending on the situation this may be worth a shot.

The uncomfortable look someone gets on their face like they'd rather be anywhere else in the world (or terribly bored) means you need to move on. They are either totally bored or feel deeply trapped with you. Your job isn't to read that person's mind; it's to read the face and body language of the person you are talking to.

> You don't have to try and sell to someone that wants nothing to do with you.

If someone is not entertained and engaged in the conversation with you, why would you keep wasting your time with them? You can go find someone that would be really interested in what you have to say! That is the beauty of the networking event. There are so many people there that you never have to worry about convincing someone that doesn't want to be convinced.

You don't have to try and sell to someone that wants nothing to do with you. Find someone that you like that likes you and you'll be one step closer to having a solid referral base.

It is always better to talk to five people and find one awesome person than to latch on to the first person you talk to and suffer through an uncomfortable, awful conversation when you obviously have nothing in common and aren't communicating together well. Even if you have to talk to ten people to find the one person, that's okay. The goal is to find at least one person at any event. If you can bond with one person per event you attend, and you only attend one networking event a week, you will have 52 genuinely fabulous people in your contact list by the end of the year. All of those people know what you do and who you do it for and are probably willing to refer you.

That is powerful stuff, just from being respectful of other people's boundaries and realizing when people don't want to be talking to you. Let people get out of your conversation if they want out, because they aren't the people you want for your business anyway.

The Boundary Wrap-up

Bonding with others is not difficult. When you are friendly and kind, forming an emotional bond with another human being can happen in under a minute. Boundaries however, are difficult. You need to know where you stand with others at all times. An easy way to do this is through the amount of information someone shares with you. Do not match their level of intimacy right away.

This is important because you always want to be a little less connected to the person you are talking to than they are to you. Unless that is, you find you are quickly progressing from networking acquaintances to legitimate friends. That's okay if it happens, but don't force it by being overly intimate with someone.

> You need to know who the gossips, leeches, and crazies are before you share...

You need to know who the gossips, leeches, and crazies are before you share at this level. There are a few people in the big city that have told me things I never wanted to know. I mean, really, really, really did not want to know. I don't share this information with others, but I have heard the same story from other people as well. They told someone they shouldn't have and now the whole city knows about this awful thing that happened. It's attached to the person until someone else slips up and tells a story to the one person that tells too many people.

If your personal story is part of your brand (if you're a life coach, or work for a trauma center, or your business can be seen as created due to this traumatic event) then it can be part of your brand. If your business has nothing to do with what happened to you...keep it to your immediate friends, not your extended friends and networking acquaintances.

When in doubt, use discretion. If someone asks you point blank if something has happened to you, use your judgment – if you've gone over your boundaries already this should be easy – if it is not in your boundaries, just say something like, "That is a logical question, but I think the real question is what are people doing to help fellow victims?" That gets the pressure off of you and on to how people can help people. Generally people can talk about what others should do all night. However you need to answer to let them know that you aren't offended they asked...but that now is not an appropriate time to talk about it.

CHAPTER 15
The Call to Action

If you have ever read an advertisement and seen "Buy Now!" at the bottom or "Quantities Limited! Purchase today!" you have seen a call to action. These are very in-your-face examples, and becoming familiar with the call to action is great because once you understand it, you'll notice more subtle examples almost everywhere.

People love to buy things and they love to be sold to.

Really, even if you think you hate being sold to, think back on experiences where you felt really good about buying – what did the person selling you that thing do? It was probably very subtle, you probably think they were just answering your questions – but they were doing it in such a way that every question you asked was bringing you closer to making a purchase.

What you want to do for your company (or career) is to develop a few different calls to action you can end your conversations with.

Here are a few examples:

- Thank you so much for spending the time and getting to know me. I really appreciate you, and am thrilled that one more person knows I'm looking to be a personal banker in Chicago.
- Wow, you are so interesting, is there any way we can have lunch and I can learn more about you and maybe we see if there is a way we can help one another?
- Thank you for the business card, do you mind if I put you on my newsletter list to keep in touch with you more effectively?

You see the different calls to action are for different circumstances. From keeping in touch to having lunch, if the person you're talking to at a networking event is someone you want to know better, you need to speak up and suggest how you can further the relationship.

If you leave it all up to everyone else, you'll quickly find yourself at the whims of a few people. You need to be the master of your own vessel. Steer your own ship. (Insert your own deep and meaningful analogy here.)

If someone seems very interested in your product or service, you can ask them while you're still in conversation, "Does this sound like something that would make your life easier?"

There is no rule that says you can't close a deal at a networking event. The only reason I don't recommend it is that people generally aren't in that place when they're networking. They go to networking events to meet people and avoid getting sold to. But if your company knocks their socks off, by all means, go in for the sale.

> ...if the person you're talking to at a networking event is someone you want to know better, you need to speak up and suggest how you can further the relationship.

The key is to get to know enough folks at these events that you start being able to read people.

Also, when someone is interested in what you do, make sure you don't start monopolizing the conversation. Ask questions, let them share too. It's about going back and forth between the two of you (or the group) not all about how cool your company is.

Even if, when you give your call to action, the response is "No, I don't think I'm interested" or "I don't know anyone looking for what you do" – don't just blow them off and move on. Just because they don't know someone today doesn't mean they won't run into someone at the next networking event that needs exactly what you have to offer.

Your goal is to get into that other person's mental contact list. If they say, "No," respond with something like, "That's okay, I'm just thrilled I had a chance to meet and talk with you." Then they don't feel like you just pumped them for information and when they weren't useful you blew them off. They feel like you were happy to meet them for who they are, because you were and told them so.

CHAPTER 16
The Exit

So you've gone to the networking event, and you've met some people and exchanged some business cards. Go you! Things look like they might be starting to wind down, some people have left already and everyone is in a more relaxed place since they know they have pretty much met everyone they are going to meet that day.

This is a perfect opportunity to find the person you bonded with most during the event and double-checking with them about making plans at a later date.

If you are already in the middle of a great conversation when you notice things starting to wind down, you can ask the person you're talking to if they want to continue the conversation over lunch, dinner, or drinks depending on the time of day. You can also wrap up the conversation by saying, "This has been such a great conversation, can we schedule a time to get back together to continue it?"

You want to try and extend the conversation with people you met that you think would either make perfect clients or that you think you might be able to refer to others. There are a million reasons why you might want to get to know someone a little better. The key is to ask them if they would like to continue the conversation.

Last but not least – do not be the last to leave the event. The only exceptions are if you know the person who is running the event is going out afterward and you're going with them, or if you are a volunteer at the event. You want to make sure the perception is not that you have no place else to be than the networking event. If you are standing there wondering what you should do next, and things are winding down, find a couple people to say goodbye to, look for opportunities to extend the conversation at a later date...and leave.

The exit can be where people who don't know better look around like they are lost, and seem a little desperate. You don't want people to think you are desperate...so don't let that happen.

Of course if one of the people you bonded with at the networking event is a vendor, by all means you can offer to help them pack up as an excuse to get to know them better, but if they say they don't need help, don't keep hanging around. It's not necessary, and can work to your detriment in a networking situation.

CHAPTER 17

On the Fly and Off the Cuff

The modified elevator speech

An elevator speech is traditionally a 30-second or so speech about your business, what you do, who you can help, and who you work with. It is generally boring and uninspired.

> Modifying an elevator speech so you can weave it into a conversation (however short) isn't as difficult as you might think.

I hate elevator speeches □ both giving them and listening to them.

It's called an elevator speech because (in theory) you should be able to explain what you do for a living in the time it takes to go down or up in an elevator.

I don't know about you, but if I'm stuck in an elevator with someone I'm not going to hammer them with facts about my business. I'm not even going to hammer them with benefits of my business. I'm going to have a short conversation with the person about what they do and then directly relate what I do to how it could benefit that individual. Modifying an elevator speech so you can weave it into a conversation (however short) isn't as difficult as you might think.

You need to make a list of the things your company does, and then you can use those individual answers when they are appropriate in the conversation. If they tell you they are an accountant, go to answer four, "My company helps accountants manage time more effectively so they can get home at night and have more of a life. What do you do for fun?" Or even, "I have four years of accounting experience. I love the field, how long have you been working as an accountant?" No matter what your answer, end with a question so the other person has a reason to keep talking to you.

A traditional elevator speech will only keep you talking *at* someone for thirty seconds. Your goal should be to keep the other person so interested in what you do, and having such a good time answering questions and having a conversation they are late to their next appointment.

Which conversation would you rather have?

The modified elevator speech is great to practice on friends, family, or even networking buddies! It helps them know more about what you do so they can refer your services, as well as gives them a chance to practice back on you and improve their networking skills.

The modified bumper sticker speech

The "Bumper Sticker" speech is usually a one-or two-sentence quick conversation opener. Usually vague and boring it forces the person to ask "What does that mean?" So you can pretend you got permission to drone on about your company.

Example: Instead of saying, "I design business cards." You would say, "I extend a company's brand as far as the eye can see."

My personal mantra is simplicity. My great-grandmother always said, "It is easier to be good than to be simple." A lot of business owners are really good at what they do, and when they explain what their company does, they do so with jargon and buzzwords and make it difficult for someone to understand what they mean unless they are in the same industry.

You need to find a way to explain what you do quickly and in an engaging way without being vague.

Business owners who are vague are not seen as business owners that will succeed. It is assumed they are new and don't have enough experience to explain what they actually do.

Your job as a smart, networking-savvy business owner is to find a way to make your two sentences clear and fun, then throw a question on the end so that the person you're talking to answers a question instead of forcing them to ask you more about what you do when they may not want to.

Example:

"I design the most fabulous business cards that allow for writing space while still being cutting edge. Do you ever write on your business cards?" Even if the other person says, "No" you have an opening to discuss the benefits of writing on someone's business card. You can have a conversation, and the other person now understands that writing on business cards is a great idea. Guess who they will think of when they tell their friends this new tidbit of information? Yep, they'll think of you.

That conversation will go something like this, "Did you know you should write on business cards? I had no idea, but this business card designer told me. She really knows her stuff when it comes to business cards." Someone in her group might even ask, "Oh, can I have her name, because I could use an update to my design."

You need to find a way to explain what you do quickly and in an engaging way...

...Please, don't be vague.

Whereas if you just said something about extending the branding, they would have asked "What does that mean?" You would have explained what it meant and they would have said, "Okay, thanks" and moved on. No referrals, no good times, no stories, no conversation.

How boring! Please, don't be vague.

I make it a point not to ask anything further if someone says something vague to me and I know my networking friends all do the same thing. We all believe if you can't tell us what you do in two sentences, we probably don't want to talk to you. I worry that's how they'll communicate in general...and I don't want to work with someone that is vague and makes me do all the question asking on a project.

CHAPTER 18

Keeping in Touch

Maintain connections for success

Even the most successful networker will eventually fail if they don't have a plan to follow up with the people they've met at events.

It is not enough to meet someone once, bond with them, and never speak to them again. The easiest way to keep in touch with people is to continue networking, and say hello to the people in the room that you have met before.

If you remember what they do but don't have a name to go with that, just say, "Hello, good to see you again, how is my favorite _____ ?" It re-establishes rapport quickly and effectively. Even if someone else walks up that you know you can introduce them as the best

_____ in the room, you don't have to worry about the name.

If you really need to use their name or want to remember it, you can always say, "You market your business so well, I can remember what you do but your name is completely not coming to me right now!" It is okay to forget someone's name as long as you remember what they do. The compliment also helps smooth things over so they just tell you what their name is and you can move on from there.

If you remember someone's name but not what they do, that's okay, you can introduce them to someone else and say, "Leslie, this is Suzie...Leslie, tell Suzie what you do...you explain it so much better than I do!" Again, the compliment smoothes things over and lets Leslie know what her next move is. Helping Leslie so she can tell someone new what she does is far more important to her than you remembering what she does. Plus it gives you a refresher on the spot.

People tend to stay in the same networking circles, so as long as you are hitting the different groups you've met people in about once a month, you can keep your connections fresh.

If you find that you aren't going to be able to network in person for a while, you have your list. The people that have signed up for your e-mail list plus the people you've asked if you can put them on your list. (If people have said while networking they do not want to be on your list, put a mark of some kind like an "X" on the business card so you know not to add them! Don't spam people!) Now is the time to send out a newsletter via e-mail to all of your contacts.

Don't use the newsletter as an excuse to talk all about you and your company only and bore everyone on the receiving end of your newsletter to tears. Do you know a Networking Buddy™ that has a sale happening on their Web site? Put that in the newsletter!

The follow-up plan

You should have some idea of your follow up strategy before you go out and get to know a bunch of people.

But you know what? No one is perfect, and when I started networking I didn't have any kind of a follow up plan. You need to keep your personal limitations in mind. Some resources to help you to get around those personal limitations are: Are you a forgetful person? Use www.iwantsandy.com to remind you to follow up with people.

- Use a contact management system like www.highrisehq.com to keep track of everyone's information as well as notes on calls you have with people.

How often you need to follow up is determined by the person you're talking to. If you talk once a month and are getting along swimmingly, then you're doing fine. Some people you may only need to talk to every few months. The gauge is generally if you call someone and they either have trouble remembering you, or pretend they don't remember you, or ask you "Hey stranger, where have you been?" You need to follow up more often.

Alternately if you call and someone says, "Oh wow, I feel like I talk to you every day!" Or anything else that sounds like a "we talk too much" signal, dial it down a notch and call a little less frequently.

You also want to make sure you're setting realistic expectations. When you only have 10 contacts you can call once a week and check in – when you have 100 contacts, you won't have time to run a business and call every contact weekly. If you start weekly and then drop down to monthly, that might not go over well with everyone. You don't want people to think you're getting in touch less because you decided you like them less or don't want to keep in contact.

The best way to avoid this is by having systems in place beforehand, or even letting people know via newsletter that you have had a lot of new contacts come in, and even though you love your old contacts more because they have been with you longer, you just can't keep up with it all.

People understand and will be happy for your success, as long as they don't feel they had a hand in that success and you're dumping them on the side of the road for shiny new contacts!

Honesty is the best policy. It is okay to be overwhelmed as long as you have a plan in place to make sure you don't continue to be overwhelmed.

Follow-up Systems

Goodness knows I didn't invent the concept of following up. In many businesses follow up can be the difference between success and having to close up shop.

I'm not a "reinventing the wheel" kind of girl, so instead, what I have are a few suggestions for creating, maintaining, and keeping track of your follow-up systems.

- **Get Clients Now!** A 30-day plan with worksheets and everything laid out in a clear, simple format. It is not too overwhelming, but not overly simplified, either. You can target your follow-ups in different ways, and choose your follow-up activities from a menu. This one is my favorite, and it works – I know that firsthand!

- **90-Day Dash** is a program that focuses on more long-term success. You can redo it quarterly as needed. It focuses on how you "touch" a prospect (by mail, e-mail, voice, or in person). Many systems suggest the same type of touch three times, but it usually takes six to seven touches in several different forms before prospects become clients.

- **Franklin Covey** If you know how you want to follow up and with whom, use an organizer like the Franklin Covey system to keep track of who you need to follow up with and for what reason.

Whatever system you choose, the only thing you have to do is stick to it. It sounds easy, I know, but you have to conquer those fears of calling people that you don't know as well as your friends and think of something to have a conversation about. It can be tough, and when things are tough they become more difficult to focus on. Suddenly you find yourself with a shoebox filled with business cards of people you've never gotten in touch with. You probably haven't thought about them for six months to a year, and they haven't thought about you.

Don't let this happen to you! Even if you just contact one person a day by phone, e-mail, or sending a note on fun stationary in the mail – it is far better than doing nothing at all. As long as you keep talking to people and keep communicating, you will be in people's minds and on their lips.

Calling your Host/Hostess

making people angry is a really big deal...

Did you have a chance to meet the person that hosted the networking event? Call the next day and tell them what a success you thought it was. Were you a vendor at someone's home party, trade show, or vendor fair? You better call and say thank you for the opportunity.

Not making people angry is a really big deal in networking. Making people feel appreciated is an even bigger deal.

People have feelings, and the minute you forget that you will wonder where all your networking buddies went. You won't be asked back for things. You will become a social pariah, because nobody likes impolite people.

So if you think your manners may not be up to par, or you have trouble with the "Golden Rule" (do unto others as you would have them do unto you – for those that may be rusty) you need to brush up on those skills because people do want to hear from you. They do want to know how their event was for you. If they don't hear from you, you're still sending a message to them loud and clear. You are sending the message that you don't appreciate the effort they made to hold a nice event for you.

Making someone feel unappreciated is the fastest way to undo all the effort you have made thus far in your networking efforts.

The Case for Gifting

When I do get referrals from people I've networked with, there are two vendors I use to send a thank you gift to the person that referred them. I don't wait until after I've been paid. I send over the gift as soon as the new client has signed a contract and I start work.

It may not be a popular opinion, but I firmly believe you should find a product to give to the people who refer people to you. Gift cards are tacky and show you didn't think for one minute before sending one. Besides, then you have to put an actual dollar value on the gift. At least with truffles or wallets or something tangible the price doesn't matter quite so much.

- **Truffles.** I go to Katherine-Anne Confections for truffles. She has my credit card information on file and I just send her an e-mail with the name, address, and a note I want sent and violá, a box of handmade truffles with packaging that is fair trade and sustainable arrives at the referrer's door! When I call them to follow up and see if they received the gift I double check dietary status and preferences and make a note in my contact manager so I know for next time what to send. (Katherine-Anne Confections also carries homemade caramels, so really, unless they just don't want a food product I know that I'm safe.

- **Ögon Wallet.** I work with a lot of fashionable people, and find that these metallic wallets available at Lucky Day Boutique are perfect for the non-foodie types. They're great to use as a business card holder. Practically indestructible and waterproof – they keep cards safe. People appreciate that, because it's thoughtful.

- **Red Envelope.** This company has been a gift giver's paradise for a long time. It is an old standard when it comes to giving gifts to your referral givers.

Don't send the same gift every time...

The gift you send should take into account how consistent the referrer is as well as how large the client is.

Don't send the same gift every time - it just gets boring no matter how fun, quaint, or wonderful the product is. Make a list and rotate, using your contact manager to make a note of what you have already sent to that referrer. Once you get the hang of it, this should be fairly automatic. You can also delegate this kind of work to a Virtual Assistant.

CHAPTER 19
What Not to Do

This is going to be the fun chapter. If you read only one chapter in the whole book...read this one!

Even if you have trouble incorporating the tips and tactics from the previous chapters in your networking...even if the only thing you do is to stop your bad networking habits...you will be in a better position than you were before you cracked Non-toxic Networking open.

Normally I try not to be negative. You will notice that most of this book is about the great things you can do in order to bring more clients, friends, and associates into your circle. You'll make friends and you'll learn things.

But there are just a few things that I feel we really need to cover because they can blow it for you, and neither one of us wants you to fail when you go out there and network!

- **Being Clingy**. If you are utilizing a Networking Buddy™, or even if you've just met someone at a new networking event...don't be clingy. Just because you went to the event with someone, doesn't make them your date and you should not treat them like they are. Work your way around the room. It's been said before, but it bears repeating: Your Networking Buddy™ is there to give you a mental security blanket, not a physical one.

- **Being rude, unfriendly, or making jokes at the expense of others**. My friend Lola went to a networking event and there was a girl waiting outside who my friend mistook for someone else. My friend called this woman by the wrong name, and the woman did not correct her and went into the event with her and used her as a Networking Buddy™. Although I would recommend correcting someone and introducing yourself; in itself this is not a big deal. It got the new girl into the event.

  But here is where it all went horribly wrong.

Through dinner the new networker made my friend the butt of multiple jokes in an attempt to create her standing with the group. She said things like "Oh, she's been calling me the wrong name for weeks!" and laughing at her own joke; insulting my friend Lola in an attempt to "get in" with the group. This is never, ever a good plan. What the new networker did not know is that the group they were at held Lola in very high regard. I can assure you they will never use the new girl's services, because she used insulting humor toward a veteran to try and seem cool.

Be Yourself.

- **Not being yourself (that is, trying to be someone else).** If you're acting fake, someone's going to spot it. You can pretend you're not nervous, but don't pretend to be someone else. Answering questions the way you think they should be answered instead of just answering them as who you are is going to be a problem. Everyone can be bland, everyone can be agreeable. Being yourself is the only thing you have that's going to set you apart from everyone else. Own yourself. Be yourself.

Find the people who like who you are. When I began networking I was this friendly, awful caricature of who I really am. I tried not to be too opinionated. I tried to be polite to everyone and not disagree. No one remembered who I was. I became part of the scenery. When I said, "To heck with it" and was myself...everyone remembered who I was and people wanted to work with me □ people really liked. People do business with people they like, but if you don't show them who you are, they won't know who you are to know if they like you or not.

- **Being generally unpleasant.** Don't be a know-it-all. Don't lie. Don't be snotty. Don't be judgmental. Do NOT, under any circumstances, have a conversation where you don't let the other person get a word in edgewise. All of these will get you labeled as someone no one likes.

- **Trash talking (AKA "talking smack").** There are some networkers I know that bond with each other over negative experiences with vendors or fellow business owners. This is scary, because you're forming a negative bond with people. Remember, if someone constantly talks about other people to you in a negative way, you'll never know what they're saying about you to someone else.

- **Blowing someone off.** Did you say you were going to meet a Networking Buddy™ at an event? Did a better offer come your way? It had better be astronomical because Networking Buddy™ relationships aren't friendships and they don't come with the promise of forgiveness for mistakes. If it is a better networking event, consider calling your Networking Buddy™ and inviting them. If it isn't something amazingly good...you may want to skip it. Your friends are going to love you forever, your business relationships are not as strong (not in the beginning anyway). You need to have your priorities straight. If you really can't attend, you need to pick up the phone and call, no matter how uncomfortable it makes you. You need to be honest and upfront with your Networking Buddy™ and hope for the best. Don't lie.

> You are going to meet tons of people while you're networking.

- **Make an emotional connection with someone and disappear.** You are going to meet tons of people while you're networking. If you've reached the point that you aren't keeping in touch as regularly as you would like, consider starting an e-newsletter to keep in touch with your contacts.

Help them find more networking events to attend where they know someone already. You need to focus on providing value to people you have met already but may not have taken the relationship farther than the occasional check-in. You can meet again at another networking event and they'll be able to start a conversation with you by thanking you for letting them know about the event. If you start an e-mail newsletter, make sure you aren't just pushing yourself on your list. Provide value through an article, links to online resources, or other networking events. Make it an e-mail people want to read, not something they feel is spam.

CHAPTER 20
About Referrals

I know people who say they are experts and don't know the first thing about what they do.

I know business owners that are not successful but coach others toward success.

In an effort to be a resource for your contacts, you may be tempted to refer people you don't know or haven't worked with. Before you refer anyone you don't know do one of two things:

1. Tell the person you're giving the referral to that you have no knowledge of the person's skills, so you're not taking responsibility for the quality of work. This shouldn't be said in a tight, serious voice. Make it light, make it friendly, but make

sure they know that the business card or contact information is only one step above getting the name out of a phone book.

2. If someone is looking for a referral, tell them you'll get right back to them, and then do a search for the person you're about to refer. See what they've said around the Internet, or call former clients if they are listed on the potential referral's Web site. The extra ten minutes of legwork will either get you out of giving a bunk referral, or give you backup for your referral when you talk to the person who was looking for a name. Either way, you look good.

> Never give your buyer list, friend list, or e-mail list to a pushy salesperson...

The best way for everyone to talk about you is to be a referral source for your potential clients and networking buddies. The worst way for everyone to talk about you is to give random, bunk referrals and back them with your name. Never give your buyer list, friend list, or e-mail list to a pushy salesperson that you are just trying to get off of your phone and out of your life.

That will not end well, I assure you.

CHAPTER 21

On Gossip

Get Ready to Have a Very Strong Opinion

I don't think there is anything wrong with gossip.

Have you stopped talking at the book? Good, let's continue. The fastest way for two people (of any gender) to bond is over stories about other people: business owners bonding over mutual acquaintances, having a little "sit down" over business disasters in the making or in the past, who won the local karaoke contest at the Village Fair.

There is a fine line between bonding and maliciousness, however. If you don't know where to stop, you better not start. There are gossips everywhere, and they come in both sexes. Some are nasty manipulative people and practically evil. Some are just people that like to tell stories about other business owners and don't have a malicious bone in their body.

Only you can determine who is who, and you need to be able to determine it on the fly when you're talking.

When you tell your story, will the person you're telling use it as leverage? They may think it will make them look good by tattling on you for telling a story? Or will they take the point you used the story to make and be a better business owner for it? The answer to those questions can make or break your networking efforts.

Me? I try to always focus on positive stories, and I'm lucky because my networking buddies always have great stories to share about contacts they made or compliments they have received on work I did for them.

Sure I have the one story about a client that didn't pay the bill...but unless someone is my friend they don't know who the client is.

What is gossip?

Is it only gossip if someone knows who the person being talked about is? Is it gossip to tell a factual story out loud? What if that story could help someone else from making a bad financial decision? It gets sticky.

> There is a fine line between bonding and maliciousness

Here is a story:

Jane rents a booth at an expensive event. She then talks to Sally who really wants to split the booth and the cost with Jane. Sally never shows up to the event and doesn't call Jane either. Now, after the event, Sally calls and tells Jane that since she wasn't at the show, she won't be paying for her half of the booth, and says she hopes Jane understands her position. The event is over already. Sally didn't give Jane any time to find another vendor to pick up the space and the bill in place of Sally. Now Sally won't pay, and the amount of the booth, while substantial to a small business, isn't big enough to make small claims court worth it. Plus, there was no signed contract, just a verbal agreement.

Would Jane sharing that story be gossip? Is retelling that story here gossip, or is it a cautionary tale for other business owners that may consider splitting the cost and space of a vendor booth with Sally?

Would you want someone to warn you, or would you rather not know it happened?

Does it all depend on the situation? How would you feel about the following scenarios for retelling the story:

1. Jane tells everyone she encounters about it, no matter the situation.
2. Jane makes it a point to tell only people Sally knows and who may eventually share a booth with someday.

3. Jane only tells it when/if someone asks her about sharing a booth with Sally.

4. Jane uses the story as a general example when anyone asks her advice about being a vendor at an event, but doesn't name names.

I realize there are more questions than answers in this section, but the answer to the question of gossip is going to be different for everyone that thinks about it. What you need to know is where your boundaries are, what you feel comfortable with sharing, and what you feel comfortable having others share with you.

As an effective networker, you are a good listener, and there will be many, many stories told to you that you would rather not know. Do you listen and keep it to yourself? What if it directly relates to someone you know?

You need to know where you stand on these questions before you get into a situation where you make an impulsive decision that is out of character for you, and pay for it with your integrity.

Oh, and negative, nasty gossip that has no basis in fact and only exists to drag someone down – that's never okay.

CHAPTER 22

On Business Cards

The care and keeping of business cards can be handled in many different ways.

What is most important is that your system works for you and allows you to use the cards for follow-ups and referrals, as you need them.

There are little leather folios that hold either 48 or 96 business cards depending on whether you put one in each slot of if you put two cards in each slot back to back.

Do you write on your business cards? If you do, putting them back to back may obscure important information on the card.

You can also get a business card scanner that will automatically input the information from the card into your customer relationship management program. This helps with follow up as well if you are prepared to make that kind of investment for your networking success.

Store your business cards in a safe place. These are the spoils of networking war! Okay, networking isn't a war, it's more like a buffet, but calling business cards your doggie bag doesn't sound as appealing.

However you choose to store them, make sure you are following up with these potential clients, customers and networking buddies that you have met in person at networking events. Here is some basic business card etiquette:

- **Don't shove your business card at someone the moment you meet them.**
- **Wait until they hand you a business card or ask them if they would like to exchange cards.**

Have a conversation with someone before you give them your card. If you can, write something on the card for the person before handing it over. This way they will be more likely to remember who you are because when they see the handwriting on the card they'll remember you writing it down for them.

The more someone remembers who you are, the more likely it is they will remember what you talked about. When they remember who you are and what you talked about, they won't be surprised one bit when you make a follow up phone call to see how they've been.

- **Don't put a business card on everyone's chair.**

If people can't put a face to the name on the card, they're more than likely just going to throw it away.

Brochures, business cards, or any other paper material you have to market your business should not be given to people without talking to them first. When someone leaves the room temporarily to go to the restroom, that should not be seen as the perfect opening to leave your travel company's magazine on the chair they temporarily left vacant.

Talk to someone and connect well enough to give them a business card. Perhaps the next time you see them at an event you can move up to the magazine. Baby steps are essential to forming lasting relationships, you can't just hand them a bunch of promotional materials with no prior relationship and think that's going to make a sale.

- **Don't assume that because someone gave you a business card they want to be on your e-mail list.**

Ask them in person or send them an individual e-mail asking if they mind being put on your list. Do something to give them a chance to give you permission or decline the offer.

If you just add people from business cards to your e-mail contact list, you run the risk of someone reporting you as a spammer to your e-mail company. When that happens your account can be blocked, Your Internet connection can be at risk, and you can get in a lot of trouble.

> When that happens your account can be blocked, Your Internet connection can be at risk...

To make sure this doesn't happen, ask someone if they mind being put on your list. Always use a company to send your e-mails that has an "unsubscribe" link at the bottom of the e-mail. That way if you do send something and the recipient decides they don't want it they can easily choose not to receive it again.

Respecting others is the easiest way to make sure they want one of your business cards. Asking someone if they'd like a brochure or magazine is the best way to give more information to people who expressed interest. When someone has asked a few pointed questions about what your company provides, that is the proper time to hand them a brochure, magazine or other marketing materials.

If you keep your ears open, and listen to the person you're having a conversation with, you will begin to notice the cues that let you know when it is time to hand over a business card that they will keep and store for future reference.

CHAPTER 23

Now That You Know Everyone

Okay, it may be physically impossible to know everyone, but there will come a time when you know enough people that it *feels* like you know everyone.

This is a dangerous time in the life cycle of the networker. Once you feel like you know everyone you are far more likely to think you can start relaxing. You might want to let your referral machine run on autopilot for a while and take a break from all the events and the meet and greets.

Be careful!

Be careful! You need to be aware that your referral network is a fickle thing.

It may be bringing you many referrals this quarter, but next quarter it just isn't producing the same results. You need to stay out there, in the public eye, reconnecting with your contacts in person.

Stay focused. Don't lose sight of your networking plan. If you have succeeded in your plan, and met your goals...that means it is time to set new ones!

Remember, if you stop networking and people from your network stop networking, there is no one out there talking about you and your company.

SECTION FOUR
OTHER BITS AND PIECES

CHAPTER 24

Fifteen Fabulous Tips to Keep in Mind When You're Networking

Here are fifteen additional things to keep in mind while you are networking. They will help you keep on top of your game as you become an expert non-toxic networker.

1. Everyone is human. Don't forget it.

Just because someone has the best business façade in the world it does not mean they are somehow better than you are. Everyone puts their pants on one leg at a time; everyone has days they just want to go back to bed.

If you treat everyone as if they are equal to you, you will go farther than kowtowing to someone you think is important when they probably just want to have a normal conversation. That does not mean to treat them disrespectfully, treat them like someone you like and respect.

2. People are at networking events to meet people.

You are one of those people! Not the guy three seats down, not the woman by the drinks, not the older man by the snacks. They are there to meet you, so introduce yourself already!

3. Refer People

If someone does great work for you, tell everyone about it. When you refer others it shows that you appreciate your fellow business owners. It is a sign of respect. It also lets the person you are talking to know that if they do good work for you, you will refer them too.

4. Forge your path based on logic, not trends

You can start out following someone, but in order to make a breakthrough you have to be able to disagree with the people your field consider experts. If you are following trails that have been made by others, not only will you never know where you're going, you won't even understand how you got where you are.

Starting by following is a great way to learn, but when you find that you disagree with the experts, you are coming to the breakthrough in your business that will get you where you need to be as an owner. You will have come to the sacred place where you have enough information and education from yourself, books, and other sources to make new decisions that aren't just a rehash of what's already available in the marketplace.

5.　Do not follow blindly◻ever.

Do your research, no matter how trustworthy someone seems to be. Be able to defend your heroes, or be armed with knowledge that allows you to explain (or understand) their foibles.

This is necessary in order to keep your subconscious happy ◻ because it will question your decisions as much as your friends and family ◻if not more. Researching the people you follow in your business philosophy will also allow you to learn more at a faster pace because you'll know the history of the person and business whose philosophy you are following.

Knowing how someone got to where they are is far more important than where they are in that moment you've found them.

6. **Look at everything with an open mind ▫ but without blinders.**

The "hot, new" product, package, or business everyone is talking about may seem like nothing special. Listen to what others are saying about it anyway. You never know what bit of information you will glean that you may need later for a relationship-marketing or networking based message.

You will find genius everywhere, in bits and pieces, and being able to put those bits together into something for yourself will create magic. Use other people as a guide.

Imitation is the sincerest form of flattery. With that in mind, if there is someone you know that is a networking dynamo, ask them what they're doing that is garnering such great results.

It's always a good idea to keep track of what other people are doing, both within your niche and outside of that space. You never know when inspiration will strike, so don't limit yourself to living in a bubble of no-information because you want to make sure all of your business ideas are fresh and original. Nothing you think of is truly original, and that's okay.

On the flip side of that, don't make large decisions about your products, services, or business model based on someone else's. Remember, you never know what someone else's life or business is like unless you're living it. No matter how successful someone seems to be, it's only your perception.

7.   No one has it together completely.

Anyone that is remotely intelligent, and is looked up to by the community, has had that "Emperor's New Clothes" feeling where they cannot believe they are the expert. If they haven't, you shouldn't be listening to them, because if they don't have humility along with their knowledge, there will eventually turn out to be some big flaw in that knowledge.

Freelancers almost have to talk about how successful they are – if they talk about the bad economy and not getting projects, they won't get clients at all.

In business, as with dating, desperation (or the perception of desperation) is the kiss of death. You won't get clients if they think you're too hungry for work. So every business owner you meet freaks out at least once in a while about how they got where they are, and where they are going, and what will keep them different and current next week/month/year. You are not the only one freaking out □ everyone is.

That being said, your freaking out should be done in private, not at a networking event. You don't want to be in a group of ten people and tell them all you are worried because if you don't get a client in the next month you have to get a full time job. That leaves an icky taste in everyone's mouth.

8. Building a business is really hard work.

They don't call it building because you sit on your ass all day drinking lemonade. You don't get a four-hour workweek until you've put in the work and systems and processes to have one. You really have to eat, breathe, and sleep your business for a long time to get to the point where you can outsource everything and just work a few hours a day on strategy and planning. It doesn't happen overnight, and it doesn't happen in the first year.

Not to say you shouldn't outsource, on the contrary! You should outsource as soon as possible, but within your budget.

I've come up with some of my best business ideas watching children's programming. I don't find children's programming particularly inspiring, in fact, I think it has gone downhill steeply in the last ten years or so. What keeps me having ideas is that no matter where I am, no matter what I'm doing, I'm thinking about my business. We cannot always take action when we want to for our business, but we can come up with ideas to implement at a later date. You need to be in your business and thinking of ways to make your business better more than you are right now.

9. **If you have thought about the 80/20 rule more than two times this week, cut it out.**

The 80/20 rule basically states that out of 100% of the time you spend doing something, 20% of that time is going to yield 80% of the results. So I hear a lot of people say "If I can get the 20% of the good stuff out of the way early in the day I'll know I'm going to succeed."

Yes, I get that the 80/20 rule is accurate. But I keep seeing this used as excuse for people to slack off because they've done what they feel is the amazing 20%, so now they don't want to waste time on the 80% that isn't great. That is not how the rule works. 80% + 20% = 100%. You need to work 100% of the time for 20% of your work to produce 80% of your results.

If you were originally planning on going to three networking events during the week, go to three networking events. Don't go to the first one, have an amazing time, and think that because it was amazing the other two won't have value. Do not make the mistake of thinking you think you can't possibly be that amazing twice in one week or you'll be giving up a potential opportunity.

You really have to work to get results. You have to be your best 100% of the time (or as close to it as you can be) to even get close to being able to maybe achieve true greatness. If you work for four hours and think "that was my 20% of awesomeness for the day" you should close up shop now because you stink at being a business owner.

10.   You should be the worst boss you've ever had.

You don't feel like going out tonight? You want to stay in, make popcorn, and watch an old movie? I don't know about you, but my boss (me!) says, "I don't care if you are having a lazy day today, if you aren't sick you need to get out and be productive at that networking event."

If you are sick, by all means don't network. You'll just get other people sick and everyone will blame you.

Sure you can be a nice boss sometimes, buy yourself lunch or something and reward yourself for having an amazing networking morning/afternoon/night.

But if you are letting yourself get out of events for no good reason, you should reconsider what kind of boss you are to yourself. Are you demanding the best? Do you have high expectations? I certainly hope so.

11.   Don't outsource it until you understand it.

The Holy Grail for business owners lately has been outsourcing. Get someone else to do it so you don't have to. There is a company that sells an Internet Marketing program and then trains people to actually do the work in the program. So if you give them your credit card number not only will they sell you the product, they'll sell you the people who will perform all the steps of the product for you. Talk about a hands-free business.

But if you don't know anything about it, how can you track and gauge results?

How will you know if it's being done right?

You won't.

You'll be at the mercy of a company giving you reports you may not understand giving you metrics and analytics you won't know anything about. How can that possibly be comforting? Aren't you running a business? If you outsource anything without understanding it, you're asking for problems and excuses. I'm sure it all works out okay occasionally for someone, but the odds are it won't be you and your business that everything just happens to work out for.

What does this have to do with networking, you ask? One of the things you can outsource to someone else is entering your business card entries into your customer relationship management system as well as your follow up schedule. You can even have a Virtual Assistant compile and send out your newsletter to all your contacts.

But if you don't understand the follow up system you have chosen, you cannot expect an assistant to understand it either. You'll end up with confusion and missed follow up calls. That does not bode well for converting those networking prospects into clients.

So understand it first, and then outsource it!

12. Networking is everywhere and everyone is your client.

Going to the coffee shop this morning? The person behind you in line might be your next client...so how about remembering to brush your teeth before leaving the house!

Running out to pick up dinner at the supermarket? Uh oh...the person you bump into next to the peas might be a potential vendor. If you want to be a successful business owner, you need to take these golden networking opportunities whenever you can to learn about the people around you in random situations.

You need to brush your hair and teeth before you leave the house. You need to remember that everyone is a potential Networking Buddy™ or client. If you go out looking a mess and acting badly, and three months down the road you find yourself giving a presentation to that person you pushed in front of in line somewhere...they're not going to hire your company, because people don't work with people they don't like.

The reason these random networking moments are so powerful is that people are not closed off to sales when they are at the grocery store. People put up walls at networking events because they know they are talking to people who want to sell them things and services. So they are on their guard. At the Starbucks no one is on guard and if you do strike up the "What do you do?" conversation they will be more open to hearing about your business.

13. Don't just treat your customers well.

You may not be the only one in your company networking. You may have a secretary, an employee, a competitor, a vendor, or any other number of people that directly know you who are networking in the same arena or similar ones as you are. If you treat the people around you badly, they are going to tell other people, and those people may not want to give you the time of day because they heard bad things about you.

While I recommend hearing both sides of the story in every situation, not everyone follows this advice. You don't want your temper to be how people know you when all you've done is walk in the front door and taken a seat and the networking event table!

14. Deliver your best quality every time, over time, and on time.

If you utter the words "it's good enough," do it over, fix it, or scrap it. You cannot deliver a half-assed product every now and then without risking the integrity (that is, the very existence and sustainability) of your company.

Negative stories spread way faster than positive ones. You will give someone an "almost ok" product and find two weeks later at a networking event someone you've never heard of before questioning your production methods.

Just because you know the name of the person you are shipping a not-so-great product to, you do not know the names of all the friends and associates of that person. You do not know who they talk to, gossip with, network with, or speak in front of.

If you do not strive for quality every time, in every interaction, and at every crossroad □ you will eventually find (probably sooner rather than later) you have told the one person that has contacts and connections beyond your wildest dreams to go take a hike because they got a sub-par experience with your company and it is easier for you to tell them to get lost rather than fix the issue.

APPENDIX
Fun With Forms

The key questions asked within the book are summarized here, into some forms that are easy to fill out. By the time you have these short, easy forms filled out, you'll have a pretty good idea of what you will be saying to the next person you meet at a networking event.

Going through this exercise is your first step. The next step is to use the information you build from the forms and take that information to your next networking event. Once you're there, meet a few people and look for a Networking Buddy™ to help you expand your network.

Above all, try to have fun! People who see you enjoying yourself at a networking event are far more likely to walk up and talk to you. Even if they don't, they'll know you have confidence and when you walk up to talk to them, they'll be far more receptive to your conversation and message than if you were being a mope and you wandered up to them with your head down, staring at the ground.

People will like you. People will want to get to know you. Your job is to not be pushy. Have real conversations; make real connections and share about your business without making the other person feel pressured or creeped out. I care about your networking success. So if you still have further questions, visit us at www.nontoxicnetworking.com and see what else we have that can help you out. You can even send me an e-mail if you have a question.

Self Evaluation of Current Networking Skills

(Be honest with yourself)

	1 Poor	2 Fair	3 Satisfactory	4 Good	5 Excellent
How do you feel about talking to strangers?	☐	☐	☐	☐	☐
How are your listening skills?	☐	☐	☐	☐	☐
How are you in social situations?	☐	☐	☐	☐	☐
How are you in crowds?	☐	☐	☐	☐	☐
How do you feel about handing out your business cards?	☐	☐	☐	☐	☐
Are you clear about what you sell?	☐	☐	☐	☐	☐

When you look at the totals of Poor vs. Excellent answers you've checked, which skills rank high? How could you use those higher ranking skills to help you improve your lower ranking skills? Using what you are already good at makes it easier to improve on things you may not be so good at right now. Write down the ways you could make improvements.

Introduction Practice

Modified Elevator Speech

What are five things you can say to someone about your business that end with a question that the other person will want to answer to keep the conversation going?

Modified Bumper Sticker Introduction

Explain what you do in two sentences and end each with an open question for the other person to answer.

Assessing Your Product

Do you know what you're trying to get
people to buy from you?

What are you selling?

What is your biggest fear?

How have you asked for the sale in the past?

How does your product or service benefit your
customers?

What makes you different from your competition?

Assessing Your Personal Brand

> ### Do you know the basics of your personal brand?

What are you selling? Your fantastic skill? Your creativity?

_____

_____

_____

_____

_____

What problem does your product or service solve for the person that uses it? Does it give them more time? Does it make life easier? Is it pretty and fun?

_____

_____

_____

_____

_____

What makes you different from others that provide what you provide? Why are you better? If you think you have no competition you are wrong and need to do more research. Just because someone does something different, they may still be competition.

_____

_____

_____

_____

_____

One-Page Networking Plan

Where do I want to Network?

_____

Do I want to network online, offline, or both?

_____

Who do I want to meet?

_____

Who are people that I know looking to meet?

_____

What is the demographic I am targeting?

_____

How many events can I attend per week?

_____

What time am I at my best? Morning/Afternoon/Evening?

_____

How much money can I spend on networking per month?

_____

How many clients or customers is my goal?

_____

Do I know anyone right now I can ask to be my Networking Buddy™?

_____

Am I open to making friends, or just connections?

_____

Calendar

Use this blank calendar to enter upcoming networking events in your area. Research the schedules on the Internet, ask a friend or a Networking Buddy™, or contact your local Chamber of Commerce for a schedule of upcoming networking events in your area. Put all of the events scheduled for the month on the calendar. Now, using the types of networking events available and taking your current skill level into consideration, pick a few events to attend as practice events. If you're really afraid of your performance, pick a Chamber a few towns away and start there.

Calendar _____ 20__ __

Sunday	Monday	Tuesday	Wednesday	Thurdsay	Friday	Saturday

Personal Insight & Networking Troubleshooting

What is your biggest fear?

If someone rejects you or doesn't like you, what are they going to do?

If you are getting negative signals from someone, what can you do to get out of the situation gracefully?

Really, what do you have to lose if you begin networking regularly?

How do you ask for the sale?

Do you even bother asking for the sale or trying to set a date for drinks or to connect again with a prospect?

Are you telling your prospect how your product will benefit them, or are you telling personal anecdotes about you?

Do you know what makes you different? Are you telling others?

Do you assume someone will say no before you even talk to them? Why?

Do you feel stupid? If so why?

_____

_____

What is the worst thing that can happen? How can you deal with that?

_____

_____

Do you think you are special? If not why?

_____

_____

Do you think your business has something special to offer others?

_____

_____

Do you assume people want to know you and work with you?

_____

_____

Do you talk more than you listen?

_____

_____

Can you visualize, fantasize, or daydream that you are the most popular person in the room--the person that everyone wants to network with?

_____

_____

Are you okay going through the rest of your life being afraid of connecting with other people?

_____

_____

RESOURCES

Gift Buying

Chic Gems, Etc. www.chicgemsetc.com

Dale & Thomas Popcorn
www.daleandthomaspopcorn.com

Katherine-Anne Confections www.katherine-anne.com

Lucky Day Boutique www.luckydayboutique.com

Luxe Candles www.luxecandles.com

Ögon Wallet www.ogondesigns.com/

Red Envelope www.redenvelope.com

Business Solutions

37Signals www.37signals.com

Biznik www.biznik.com

Business & Learning www.businessandlearning.com

Dictionary.com www.dictionary.com

Facebook www.facebook.com

Franklin Covey www.franklincovey.com

Get Clients Now! www.getclientsnow.com

Highrise Contact Management www.highrisehq.com

I Want Sandy www.iwantsandy.com

LinkedIn www.linkedin.com

Meetup www.meetup.com

MySpace www.myspace.com

Professional Women's Network www.pwn.org

Squidoo www.squidoo.com

Startup Nation www.startupnation.com

INDEX

ABOUT THE AUTHOR

Jennifer Gniadecki is a freelance corporate writer and blogger. She lives in Greater Chicagoland and believes effective networking is the true secret of her success.

From blogging at http://beyondmom.com, to keeping her Corporate writing portfolio updated at http://jennydecki.com, you'll find Jennifer most at home building relationships and connecting people.

A firm believer in simplicity, you won't find her throwing around buzzwords and jargon. Jennifer believes the most powerful communication is also the easiest to understand. Her writing reflects her philosophy and her simple, powerful writing style has been used by Walmart and Hanes. She has also been quoted in Glamour Magazine, the LA Times and the Chicago Tribune.

Editors love working with Jen, because she always keeps the end goal, the reader, in mind.

From buying a car to landing a date, networking is responsible for some of the best things life has to offer. Once you understand how to network effectively, you'll see the world in a different light.